America's Digital Army

America's Digital Army

Games at Work and War

Robertson Allen

University of Nebraska Press
Lincoln and London

Acknowledgments for the use of previously
published material appear on page xii,
which constitutes an extension of the copyright page.

Library of Congress Control Number: 2017937445

Set in Charter by John Klopping.

Men are born for games. Nothing else. Every child knows that play is nobler than work. . . . But trial of chance or trial of worth all games aspire to the condition of war for here that which is wagered swallows up game, player, all.

CORMAC MCCARTHY, *Blood Meridian*

Contents

Illustrations

Acknowledgments

There are many people who deserve thanks for their contributions not only to the content of this book, but also to the encouragement they have provided throughout its writing. Miriam Kahn, Danny Hoffman, Lorna Rhodes, David Price, and Crispin Thurlow provided outstanding early feedback. Many other individuals have also influenced aspects of this book, including Henry Lowood, Rebecca Carlson, Jussi Parikka, Sverker Finnström, and Neil Whitehead. I thank Mike Zyda, Mike Bode, Jonathan Breese, and Erich Iveans for their fact-checking reviews of specific chapter drafts.

I also thank those people within the Army Game Project who were willing to open their doors to my research. This project would not have been possible without the research access granted to me by Casey Wardynski. Phillip Bossant and Mike Bode were also very generous in allowing an outside researcher full access to their game development studio. Other specific employees of the Army Game Project are numerous and unnameable. Many were very generous with their time, granting interviews, giving tours, and answering my questions. I wish to especially thank the *America's Army* game developers for accepting me, in a small way, as a member of the "team" and opening a window into their lives.

This project would not have been able to take off without necessary research grants from the National Science Foundation and the University of Washington's Anthropology Department. The Chester Fritz Endowment further facilitated preliminary writing. I owe special gratitude to the Institute for Advanced Study on Media Cultures of Computer Simulation (MECS) at Leuphana University, Germany, whose generous research fellowship support and camaraderie made the composition of this book possible. Special thanks to my fellow fellows there, Anne Dippel and Adam Page, for their conversations and advice pertaining to this book.

I thank Louis and William, whose meows have kept everything in perspective. And most importantly, Dorothy Cheng, my best critic and soundboard, who has been with me through all the gaming, researching, fieldworking, and writing.

Portions of this book have appeared previously in a variety of forms. Elements from chapters 1 and 6 appeared originally in "Virtual Soldiers, Cognitive Laborers," in *Virtual War and Magical Death: Technologies and Imaginaries for Terror and Killing*, ed. Neil L. Whitehead and Sverker Finnström (Durham NC: Duke University Press, 2013). A shorter version of chapter 2 appeared as "*America's Army* and the Military Recruitment and Management of 'Talent': An Interview with Colonel Casey Wardynski," *Journal of Gaming and Virtual Worlds* 6, no. 2 (2014). Parts of chapter 3 appeared in both "The Unreal Enemy of America's Army," *Games and Culture* 6, no. 1 (2011), and "Games without Tears, Wars without Frontiers," in *War, Technology, Anthropology*, ed. Koen Stroken (New York: Berghahn Books, 2012). Aspects of chapter 4 pertaining to the Virtual Army Experience were originally fleshed out in "The Army Rolls through Indianapolis: Fieldwork at the Virtual Army Experience," *Transformative Works and Cultures* 1, no. 2 (2009).

America's Digital Army

1   America's Digital Army

The action takes place in an oppressed yet stubborn country—
Poland, Ireland, the republic of Venice, some South American
or Balkan state . . .

JORGE LUIS BORGES, "Theme of the Traitor and the Hero"

PJ Goes to War

PJ's world is limited and intense.[1] It is confined to one large street that
is about four blocks long and filled with an array of abandoned shops,
hotels, vehicles, and restaurants. This street is bordered by smaller parallel and interconnected alleys —two to the east and one to the west. A
bright but cloudy sky casts brilliant shadows upon brownish gray buildings and shattered rubble in the streets of this city called Travnizeme.
PJ, however, gives scant attention to these details, as he knows that he
and his fellow squadmates have a critical mission to undertake. PJ's
squad leader, named TehLux[o]r, explained in the mission briefing
moments earlier that a group of Czervenian enemy soldiers is fast
approaching, escorting one of their VIPs to safety. PJ does not know who
this VIP is or why he is so important, nor is he aware of the strategic and
political implications of his mission. This information is not relevant.
He knows only that his squad's mission is to kill this VIP at all costs before
he can make it to the extraction point on the other side of the city.

Five of his squadmates, Fire Team A plus the squad leader, head west
to cover the exits from a side alley. PJ's unit, Fire Team B, is responsible
for covering the eastern sector for possible enemy VIP extraction attempts.
As two soldiers in PJ's fire team run toward stairs that will take them to
a rooftop overlooking the main street, his fire team leader, LawBringer,

calls out the full name assigned to PJ when he first joined the U.S. Army: "Perplexed Jaguar, follow me!" "Sure thing LawBringer," PJ answers. They dart north down an eastern side alleyway, up a short flight of stairs, and around several corners. LawBringer continues north down the alley at a dead run. PJ follows, but hesitates, knowing by experience that such incautious tactics are one way of getting quickly killed. Instead, PJ checks his flanks and squares off, bringing up the iron sights of his MI6A4 machine gun. He covers LawBringer's headlong sprint down the dark alley, but realizes there is little he can do to protect his fire team leader.

PJ is still a rather inexperienced soldier himself, but he understands that LawBringer is demonstrating what his squadmates have disparagingly referred to as "noob" soldier behavior. LawBringer can only learn through experience, PJ tells himself. Sure enough, as his fire team leader runs down the alley past the open back door to a hotel, PJ hears the dreaded sounds of a Czervenian Obran being fired at close quarters, and he knows that disregarding LawBringer's orders was the right decision. He watches through his iron sights as a hidden enemy soldier unloads rounds of bullets into LawBringer from inside the hotel. PJ's fire team leader falls to the ground, severely injured and incapacitated but not dead. "I can see him. He's right inside the hotel door," LawBringer communicates through PJ's headset. Moments later, though, the enemy soldier edges into the alleyway in hopes of securing LawBringer to immobilize him from taking part in further combat. In the shadows, PJ waits until the enemy is centered in his sights, then fires repeatedly. The enemy soldier falls to the ground next to LawBringer.

PJ patiently waits, thinking that perhaps there is another enemy nearby covering his fallen teammate's flanks. But PJ can hear the injured enemy soldier speaking in his own language over his communications headset, presumably calling for medical aid and informing his teammates of PJ's location: "Priypa Hesti! Enepria Verdite! Enepria Verdite!" PJ knows he needs to silence quickly the incapacitated enemy soldier, but he hesitates to kill him since this would be a severe violation of the U.S. Army's rules of engagement (ROE). ROE violations happen regularly in this particular theatre of conflict, but PJ knows that the consequences for such dishonorable actions include a prompt imprisonment in Fort Leavenworth. PJ has been there in the past and he does not want to go back. Choosing not to become a war criminal this time around, he cautiously secures the enemy soldier, an action that removes the ability to communicate with teammates or participate in further combat operations.

PJ has been listening to the tense chatter of Fire Team A's squadmates, now apparently engaged in a firefight to the west. In the meantime Law-Bringer has been bleeding severely, having been shot multiple times in the right arm, chest, and right leg. Although PJ now seriously doubts the benefit of having LawBringer as a teammate, he knows that healing him would at least get an injured teammate back into the action, if only to cause a short distraction for the enemy soldiers. It would also earn LawBringer's gratitude, increase PJ's honor in the eyes of his squadmates, and maybe even get him a medal. PJ crouches over LawBringer, and after about fifteen seconds of first aid treatment—just as he was taught during training for basic combat lifesaving—LawBringer's multiple bullet wounds are patched and he is again on his feet. The fire team leader's injuries prevent him from moving very fast, but he is an extra gun and an extra set of eyes for PJ to use to his advantage.

Two shadows of enemies almost immediately emerge from the foliage in a square to the north of the alley. "Two Czervos coming this way," LawBringer calls out, as PJ hears the report of two Obrans and the subsequent impact of bullets into both LawBringer's flesh and PJ's body armor. PJ does not pause to check on the state of LawBringer. He very likely is dead now. Instead he turns around and sprints into the hotel, away from the fast approaching enemies. He sprints up some spiraling stairs, down a hall, and into an empty room. Crouching down, his back against the wall, PJ waits. He feels like a coward, camping in the hotel bedroom like this, but if he plays it right it might just be the best strategy. He assesses his wounds: a light bullet scrape on his left shoulder, but without severe bleeding; and a direct hit to his chest, but the body armor prevented injury. His radio communication with other squadmates is still active, so he relays the vital information to the rest of the surviving U.S. Army soldiers in the area: "There are two who just came in through the back door of the hotel. One looked like he could be the VIP. I'm in the second floor, side room." "I'm on it," the voice of his squad leader TehLux[o]r, responds, "I think we're the only two left."

As he waits for the arrival of his teammate and the opportune moment to emerge from hiding, PJ reflects upon his experiences in recent weeks. It was a quick journey from boot camp to Travnizeme, but a journey that involved hundreds of deaths and failures in addition to emotional victories. PJ has learned and improved his skills with every mistake, and he has made friends—brothers in arms—for whom he would risk his life. He has already done so multiple times, and even died for them, in this theater of conflict. Several days ago he and two others were killed in this very room by a hand grenade tossed into the open window by some lucky noob Czervo.

PJ is brought out of his reveries as he hears gunfire downstairs in the hotel lobby. TehLux[o]r apparently has found one of the two enemies that had been chasing him. All becomes silent following the deafening boom of a grenade from downstairs. Maybe an enemy was killed by the blast, or maybe not. TehLux[o]r, though, is dead; his voice commo is down. PJ hears dull sounds of movement in the second floor's back room overlooking the alley. He moves quietly down the hall, readying his weapon. He turns the corner and sees the VIP facing away from the door and looking out a window. Hearing something suspicious, the VIP moves as if to turn around, but it is too late. A barrage of bullets leaves PJ's rifle and enters the head of the VIP. It is an immaculate death, clean of any bone fragments or slippery bits that would otherwise splatter out the window. Only a slight puff of red appears as the VIP ragdolls and flops to the floor.

PJ has completed the mission. Celebratory music plays as time stops in PJ's world, and the glorious, disembodied dead from PJ's squad shout in jubilation. They had all been watching the action from their purgatorial state. TehLux[o]r congratulates him: "That was awesome, man!" "Hey, thanks for helping me out," says LawBringer. Two minutes later a different scenario plays itself out in this world of alleys, and with the same respawned soldiers. This time, however, PJ isn't as cautious or lucky, and he takes a bullet to the neck. As he bleeds and audibly gasps for air, the screen turns red, then fades to black. The same alley scenario replays itself again and yet again. Perhaps the next time Perplexed Jaguar is protecting the VIP instead of trying to kill him; maybe in some lives he actually *is* the VIP. The possible permutations of this thread multiply as PJ's career in the U.S. Army expands, but the constant variables of killing and death, victory and defeat, and honor and teamwork through armed combat are all that PJ ever knows or understands.

The Army Game Project

In PJ's spectacular war story, a clear delineation of war from its representations is lacking. There are elements that point to an uncanny, inhuman element in PJ's interactions with both enemies and teammates. In fact PJ is an amalgamation of human and computer, a prosthetic extension of a human user within an online digital game. Perplexed Jaguar (i.e., PJ) was the name the video game *America's Army 3* automatically generated for me upon my first time playing the game. (Players can create their own name or go with one that is given to them.) PJ's narrative may be an overdramatic war story, but for a gamer who has temporarily suspended disbelief long enough to become immersed in this environment, PJ's experiences, and by extension the experiences of PJ's human player, are very real, embodied, and physically stimulating. Video games are part of a "magical spectacle" of stimulation and perception that involves real adrenalin rushes, real increased heart rates, and other real sensory experiences and interpersonal communications (Virilio 1989, 6). These real sensations and emotions, as well as PJ's war story, might be a novelty for many who are unfamiliar with military-themed video games; but for the tens of millions of gamers worldwide who play first-person shooting (FPS) games and other competitive games, they are not very exceptional.

Despite its unexceptional position as merely one narrative among the vast array of other virtual war stories that have been enacted within video game worlds since at least the late 1970s, PJ's story still stands out for one reason: it takes place within a public and freely accessible PC (personal computer) video game environment that has been entirely funded and produced by the U.S. Army. A hardcore player of the game *America's Army 3*, published in the summer of 2009, would be able to identify PJ's firefight as having taken place within a game scenario known as "Alley (Day Cloudy)," with the mission type being "VIP" (see fig. 1). He—most players of *America's Army* have been men—would be capable of identifying many of the rooms and doors that PJ passed and imagining the nuanced clinks of grenades and ricochets of bullets hitting cinderblocks or bricks. (Many of the game sounds were recorded from real weapons at army firing ranges.) He would intuitively understand the unwritten rules and interfaces of PC gaming that might leave many uninitiated people lost.

This hypothetical gamer playing as PJ would most likely not be in the army, nor would he be interested in joining it, even though many people who play *America's Army* are military veterans or prospective recruits. *America's Army*, after all, is an elaborate interactive advertisement for the U.S. Army. As with most ads, only a small portion of people who experience it fully buy into the product.

The army does not need or expect every player of the game to be completely persuaded to enlist, though. An *America's Army* player who, through his play experiences, comes to more readily accept the status quo of army norms, priorities, and ways of thinking about the world counts as a success as well. This is the essence of the rationale behind the U.S. military's long-term investment in entertainment and interactive technologies that possess a persuasive power, investments considered by many to be outside the sphere of what the military does or should do.

After the army released the original version of the game on July 4, 2002, for free download and online play, initial reactions saw the game more as a novelty than anything that would significantly influence the future of gaming, army recruiting, or military training. Game journalists wondered whether the military could even produce a good game in the first place, especially when one of the game's self-proclaimed (and not very fun-sounding) goals was "to educate the American public about the U.S. Army and its career opportunities, high-tech involvement, values, and teamwork" (Army Game Project 2002, 1). The appeal of "free," coupled with a compelling game design and the rising popularity of online networked competitive FPS games like *Counter-Strike*, worked in the game's favor. Numerous gamers worldwide quickly began playing it as a form of entertainment and socializing. The post-9/11 but pre–Iraq War context of the game's release further contributed to its initial success, as news media outlets persisted in implying a connection between the 9/11 terrorist attacks and the Iraqi government under the presidency of Saddam Hussein, thus justifying the Bush administration's calls to war in Iraq.[2] Playing a parallel story of the U.S. Army engaged in combat operations in a vaguely Middle Eastern setting, gamers interested in vicarious wish fulfillment found that the game's thin narrative met their desires (Li 2003).

The game continued to grow through the first decade of the twenty-first century, transforming itself into a franchise of multiple games for multiple audiences and purposes. The PC game released periodic updates and consistently ranked among the most played online games. In 2009 Guinness awarded the franchise five world records, reflecting its historically substantial influence on the evolution of interactive media and military gaming. These awards, which seem politically tailored so that only this one game could receive them, included the Largest Virtual Army (9.7 million registered users, about eight times the total size of the actual U.S. Army), Most Downloaded War Video Game (42 million downloads), Most Hours Spent Playing a Free Online Shooter (231 million hours as of August 2008), Earliest Military Website to Support a Video Game, and Largest Travelling Game Simulator.[3] Successive versions of the game, such as PJ's world of *America's Army 3* (2009), supported additional modifications designed to train army soldiers, as well as applications aiding in the development of future weapon technologies. The once small *America's Army* project whose developers were, in their own words, "flying by the seat of our pants," quickly expanded to encompass a large network of commercial and military institutions known as the Army Game Project.

The Army Game Project attempted to integrate a dynamic, and often difficult, nexus between a fast-moving knowledge economy and business contracting model, on the one hand, and the slower-moving procedures of a hierarchical military and bureaucratic government, on the other. The contrast between the lifestyles of game development work and military work could not have been starker. The project was at the forefront of the trends in "serious games" and military entertainment for the better part of a decade, and its ramifications have been widespread, spanning not only the "interactive entertainment" (i.e., games) industry, but also the growing military simulations industry and the U.S. government. In 2002, when the army recruitment rate was falling due partly to deployments in Afghanistan, the Army Game Project and *America's Army* contributed to a new push by the army to market itself to potential recruits and the public at large. It also spearheaded the development of software packages for arms development, weapons and leadership training, and post-traumatic stress disorder (PTSD) rehabilitation.

A wide network of commercial, government, and military studios in Raleigh, Los Angeles, San Francisco, Seattle, Orlando, and elsewhere designed entertainment and government adaptations of the *America's Army* game, and offices at the U.S. Military Academy and at the Redstone Arsenal military base near Huntsville, Alabama (where the platform continues to be managed), oversaw the entire project. On the interactive entertainment side, *America's Army* established contractual agreements with well-known game companies. Game industry giant Ubisoft published PlayStation 2, Xbox, and Xbox 360 versions of the game, and Epic Games licensed its commercially successful Unreal game engine, commonly used in many FPS games, to the Army Game Project. The franchise at its height included several PC and console games, an active online community of game users, two product lines of *America's Army* plastic G.I. Joe–like action figures, a coin-operated arcade game, a cell phone game, and a graphic novel series.

The *America's Army* platform was also central to a high-tech venture in Philadelphia with the Pentagon, local army recruitment centers, area high schools, the marketing company Ignited, and the Franklin Mills shopping mall, all of which cooperated in the implementation of the Army Experience Center (AEC), a two-year experimental program (2008–10) in military recruitment focusing on less-affluent, suburban, and predominantly nonwhite regions of big cities, areas that historically have been difficult for recruitment. The Army Game Project furthermore oversaw the development and implementation of a ten-thousand-square-foot "mobile mission simulator" dubbed the Virtual Army Experience (VAE), which toured throughout the United States between 2007 and 2009 to air shows, state fairs, and NASCAR events, hosting a twenty-minute immersive Disneyland-style simulated army gaming/recruiting experience.

The examples above only represent the entertainment, recruitment, and public outreach side of the Army Game Project. Other applications of the *America's Army* platform offered the U.S. military and government organizations software for weapons development, as well as for soldier training and injury rehabilitation. One software application, for example, teaches new army enlistees who have yet to go to basic training some essentials in land navigation, military map reading, and first aid. Another early government application of the software trained U.S. Secret Service agents. Other prominent "government application" examples of the game technology include a close-quarters combat simulator using live-fire ammunition and a military-convoy skills simulator, both of which are directed at training soldiers to make quick and effective combat decisions while under stress—for example, enemy gunfire.

The reasons for the existence of such a broad network devoted to the Army Game Project, as well as the benefits for the army in placing a high-caliber game in the middle of popular FPS gaming culture, were numerous. In addition to being an efficient and cost-effective marketing tool to target the enlistment of male teenagers, the game's designers intended it to reduce recruitment attrition and cheaply train soldiers through simulations of expensive equipment. In 2003 the military invested over $13,000 for each new recruit, including $1,900 in advertising. (The former figure includes the salaries of army recruiters.) The game's designers hoped that by introducing a tailored training platform for new recruits to play, which provided "a realistic intro to the Army before getting to boot camp," basic training dropout rates and the high associated costs that the army has to bear, even when a recruit drops out of basic training, would fall (U.S. General Accounting Office 2003, 11; Zyda 2004). Salary bonuses, education incentives, and an overall push by the army to market itself as an attractive career—rather than a fallback option—also played into this retention strategy.

War Games at Work

The recruitment and training through digital technologies for the *labor* of war-making is the key theme of this book, and one that recurs in multiple formats throughout the following pages. Broadly speaking I focus my investigation on three kinds of "work" that interactive technologies like *America's Army* seek to capture and control for military purposes. The first, and most basic, form of work that I examine is the work of and on the public game itself when placed in the context of its intended audience. This includes considering the kinds of persuasive messaging that the game deploys, the ways in which army management fashions and studies intended users of the game, and how the game articulates certain ideological positions (such as the imagination of national enemies) to its users. Digging deeper, I investigate how those who designed and developed the game and its marketing messages understand both *America's Army* and their own work on the project.

This kind of game work, however, is only useful to most military strategists if it can be applied to the recruitment of actual soldiers, and the work of the recruited, or soon-to-be recruited, soldier in the context of digital games is the second form of work that I examine. Although *America's Army* has done much more than support army recruitment and training, these have been the primary reasons for the persistent existence of the game platform over the course of fifteen years. The training and rehabilitation of soldiers through virtual technologies is a rapidly growing industry, and one to which the *America's Army* platform continues to contribute. While the recruitment mission of *America's Army* has, since 2009, given way to this trend, I also query the underlying rationale for why a video game was thought to be a viable project for recruitment in the first place. It may be the case that the current market of FPS and other military-themed commercial games might inadvertently be doing the work of recruitment, even as the commercial version of *America's Army* fades into irrelevancy amid much more visually compelling games that have exponentially larger fan bases, such as those games in the *Call of Duty* and *Battlefield* series that are released on a near-annual basis.

The third area of "work" on which I focus takes place on a much broader level, and it is here that the central claim of the book resides: I argue that military-funded and -themed gaming technologies like *America's Army* take part in a militarization of American society that constructs everyone, even nonplayers of games, as *virtual soldiers*, whose labor is available for deployment. I understand the term "virtual" to represent its commonly understood meaning of "the digital," but also to refer to its older meaning of *that which is not yet actualized*, that is, "potential." We are all virtual soldiers, in a sense, because actual military enlistment, or the aspiration and ability to enlist, are not the determining factors that construct a virtual soldier. Instead the conceptualization of virtual soldiers takes place at the level of institutions, such as the military. Once confined mostly to the institution of the military itself, under current post-Fordist capitalist systems the process of cultural militarization and militarized subject formation now takes place across a smoother, less hierarchical space that encompasses technologies and entertainment, structures of labor and business, and other institutions, such as prisons, schools, and religious organizations. In this way a person who does not have even the slightest desire to join the military might nevertheless be a virtual soldier. I use the labor of the *America's Army* employees as specific examples of how the process of virtual soldiering works, and then delve further to look at how my own labor as a researcher, external to the entire project, nevertheless became appropriated in certain ways. I too was (and am still) a virtual soldier.

All digital games operate and are created within systems of power. Some also challenge them, but the work of game development is always dependent on economic and political factors. In the case of *America's Army*, the project was well-funded during the lead-up to and aftermath of the invasion and occupation of Afghanistan in 2001 and Iraq in 2003. At that time the manpower and recruitment requirements of the military rose drastically, and money was easy to come by for the project. By challenging many of the more entrenched and expensive "legacy" models of recruitment, however, the project made institutional enemies— and allies—within the greater organization of the army. Following the economic downturn in 2008, the rate of recruitment to the U.S. military rose as more appealing jobs became scarce. Recruitment came to be easy, and novel solutions such as the Army Game Project saw their once relatively reliable funding extensively cut in 2009. As of 2016 the program is dramatically diminished, with an uncertain future, but the questions raised by the circulation of *America's Army* and other Army Game Project products are very much apropos in a society shaped by the economy of war, immersed in the interactive spectacles of conflict, and distracted by a pervasive overload of information.

Ethnography—both the doing and the writing—happens through the ethnographer's interactions with people, institutions, texts, and memories. It is an ongoing interpretative process; in the following pages, I present a series of moments in this process. I have chosen to examine the practices of the Army Game Project because it has a fascinating history and depth, one that reaches to the core of the militarized and technophilic American psyche and illuminates a multitude of political, economic, and sociocultural issues. Most prominent among these issues is a global trend in militarization that needs to be understood more broadly. Other issues include the changing nature of work, and how media might reinforce or challenge regimes of power. Like *America's Army*, this book is an idiosyncratic project; it is intended to be one way, and hopefully not the only way, to embark on a better understanding of the interconnected processes of militarization, entertainment, and labor in the early twenty-first century.

Fieldwork Beginnings

In what follows I relate the interconnected stories of the Army Game Project. At my field sites I have used a variety of ethnographic tools of investigation, according to what I have deemed most useful and relevant. Participant observation, a tool for data collection that involves the self-reflexive documentation of the "thereness" of the ethnographer, has been my go-to method of research. I have recorded over sixty interviews with game developers, army officers and enlisted soldiers, activists, PR representatives, and industry professionals, and have had many more informal conversations with these same people over lunch, coffee, or beer. I had my own office at the *America's Army* game development studio in Emeryville, California, for six months, where I was present throughout the workweek, sitting in on studio meetings and devoting several weeks of total game time to *America's Army*, often playing with the developers of the game during play-testing sessions. I have been the guest for numerous official tours and arranged visits at military bases, marketing and games companies, and recruiting events. I traveled to Indiana, where I spent three weeks at the state fair and Indianapolis air show, and drove to Philadelphia to play games with middle and high school kids who would visit the Army Experience Center after school. I attended two of the largest video game industry events as a member of the press, led impromptu round table discussions at the *America's Army* marketing agency, and witnessed the layoffs of over thirty people, many of them friends with whom I have stayed in contact over the years. I documented these and other modes of participant observation as data in one form or another through audio recordings, detailed written notes, document collection, photographs, or whatever other eclectic means were available and appropriate at the time.

This fieldwork journey into the heart of *America's Army* developed from a lifelong passion for video games. Although I consider myself a native player of military first-person shooting games (as well as other kinds of games), my interactions with soldiers, game developers, marketers, and government project managers were not from the point of view of an insider. I often play video games obsessively, but this did not make me a video game developer or marketer. I have family and friends in the armed forces, but I nevertheless was an outsider to all things military when I first embarked on this project. As an outsider I chose to look at the workings of the Army Game Project to trace the connections and meanings of this project across the wide spectrum of actors invested in the development, marketing, and presentation of the hybrid product known as *America's Army*.

I originally became intrigued by *America's Army* in the winter of 2005, during my first year of graduate school. I had newly relocated to Seattle after living in Japan for three years teaching English, and I was just beginning to return to my old habits of gaming, which had always been a delightful—and often necessary—antithesis to study and work for me. The American war in Iraq was coming into full swing, taking the media limelight away from the other war in Afghanistan, and George W. Bush had just been re-elected. As an anthropology graduate student in Seattle, I was surrounded by and caught up in antiwar sentiment. At the same time, I was captivated by the bourgeoning genre of commercial military-themed FPS games that were coming onto market and were, in my eyes, profiting from unjust wars. My pleasure in these games made me feel uneasy—and it was not unease at my enjoyment of the simulated violence in the games, as many may think. This apprehension was both personally and academically intriguing, and something I felt I needed to explore more deeply.

I have little patience for arguments that implicate video games as primary causes of violence or long-term aggression, especially when the news media have repeatedly scapegoated games as underlying reasons that mass shootings happen. Studies of video game "effects" (i.e., violence and long-term aggression) are usually too problematic to yield convincing results (Schreier 2013, 2015), and yet the popular myth of a verified link between video games and actual violence persists. My apprehension concerning military-themed FPS games therefore came not from the violence represented in them or from the purported effects of violent games, but in the underlying ideological and political messages that were voiced by the games that I was playing. For example the games *Conflict: Desert Storm* and *Conflict: Desert Storm II—Back to Baghdad* celebrated the 1990s Gulf War in Iraq, but were strategically released as commercial products during the period leading up to, and immediately following, the 2003 Iraq invasion (Allen 2011; Stahl 2010). These and other games and media had played directly into the Bush administration's prevailing hawkish positions in support of war, positions that implicitly and incorrectly connected the 2001 al-Qaeda September 11 terrorist attacks to Saddam Hussein's regime in Iraq (Jarecki 2005; Stahl 2007). Other seemingly innocuous games of mine, such as those in the beloved *Civilization* franchise, seemed to perpetuate colonialist settler narratives of conquest and to emphasize war over diplomacy in settling differences. These elements had always been there in the games I had played, but it was as if I had had an awakening in my moment of opposition to American war—a realization that my video games speak about war, and maybe not in ways that I entirely like.

My unease incited me to think more critically about my own gaming and inspired me to start what I envisioned as a small research project on military-themed FPS games. I began playing *America's Army* and reading more research coming from scholars in the newly emergent academic field of game studies, which was then still in relative infancy. By 2005 so-called advergames, "games for change," and the idea of using games for educational purposes had taken hold of the games industry and games research in a big way, and the overall "serious games" sector of the industry had become dominated by a military presence that included *America's Army* and other kinds of military training simulations.

I discovered that, oddly enough, the U.S. Army's original rationale for funding *America's Army* stemmed from a different kind of unease at the way commercial military-themed FPS games represented the U.S. Army and American war. While I was concerned with underlying messages in such games that seemed to support actual war through ideological themes that appeared overtly nationalistic (and often racist, colonialist, and jingoistic) in commercial military-themed FPS games, the U.S. Army felt that they misrepresented the military service in other ways. *Call of Duty*, *Battlefield*, and other commercial franchises, for example, satisfy individualistic styles of play through their design, and work against the idea that military combat units operate as a highly coordinated team. The army wanted to counteract such representations of soldiers by emphasizing teamwork, and also by working toward design choices that would deter Rambo-style "run and gun" approaches. For this reason *America's Army* deliberately designed player characters who were more physically (but not mentally and emotionally) vulnerable, who more easily take injury. (Most commercial military games, by comparison, design player health systems that tend to enable player characters to merely "breathe it off" behind a rock after taking thirteen or so bullet wounds and regain full health within seconds.) The regular depiction of soldiers who "go rogue," or who deploy "unsanctioned violence" in these and other commercial entertainment media was also a concern to army officials. They wished for portrayals of soldiers who only "do the right thing" and operate within the sanctioned boundaries of national and international law. The army furthermore wanted to portray through the video game the array of jobs and possible career paths that the army offers beyond mere combat roles, although the task of doing this through a first-person shooting game has proven to be rather difficult over the years.

Once I understood that *America's Army* had these kinds of goals, my project narrowed to just one game, but in the process it expanded past it. I quickly realized how this game was situated at an awkward and interesting spot in terms of the current milieu of war, interactive entertainment, and politics. Various parties, it seemed to me, might interpret *America's Army* in different ways according to their own predispositions. Despite the army's intentions at limiting in-game violence, antiviolence crusaders on both the left and right might tend to think of the game as reprehensible or morally suspect. When I bring up the topic of this research with many leftist acquaintances and academics with whom I otherwise typically align, people more often than not assume that I have an agenda to critique both the military and violent video games—and especially those developed by the military and targeted at youth as young as thirteen years old. For example one professor in my old department insisted to me that all such violent video games are "pornography." There is certainly a wide array of problematic elements in most any game that I think are fruitful to explore and critique, as I do throughout this book with *America's Army*. However, I did not think that it was wise to begin with this assumption for both culturally relativistic and practical reasons, since I was working to gain long-term access to military and civilian personnel working for the Army Game Project.

Instead I sought to approach this project from the starting position in the manner of classic anthropological research, withholding judgment yet maintaining a self-reflexive acknowledgment of my own predispositions and biases. With a goal of discovering how individuals and organizations understand themselves as members of the Army Game Project, I decided to contact the top of the hierarchy, not really expecting any reply or results. I emailed the project's director at West Point, an economics professor and colonel, Dr. Casey Wardynski, in the late spring of 2006. I told him that I wanted to study as an anthropologist the behind-the-scenes process of military game development, emphasizing the long-term nature of most ethnographic studies and my desire to do research in an institutional setting. Having been discouraged about the possibilities of accessing the organizations composing the Army Game Project by estranged former *America's Army* executive Mike Zyda, I doubted that the army would allow an unknown anthropology graduate student access to its game development institutions. Zyda told me in an email, "My guess is that you might have a near impossible time getting in. They tend to be very busy and wary of people studying them."[4] I was resigned to the fact that this investigation might have to be done from the outside looking in.

To my surprise Wardynski replied to my messages, and after a few more emails he invited me to his office at West Point in July 2006. As I drove along the Palisades Parkway near the military academy for the first time, the beautiful scenery of trees, mountains, canyons, and rivers seemed the last place on earth that a military base should be located. But there it was, a veritable fortress on a hill, positioned at a strategic curve in the Hudson River as it pushes its way south through the Hudson Highlands toward New York City. Leading to the main campus security gate, the buildings of the small and cozy town of West Point oozed the airs of affluence, privilege, and education.

Wardynski's workplace was at the Office of Economic and Manpower Analysis (OEMA), which he directed from 1995 until his retirement from the army in 2010. In an odd juxtaposition—or perhaps not, considering how the social sciences have historically served as arms of the military (Price 2004, 2008)—OEMA shared the same building as the Department of Social Sciences, Department of English, and the Combating Terrorism Center (see fig. 2). I arrived there twenty minutes early, walked through the building's corridors to get a feel for the layout, and sat down outside on a bench. "What the hell am I doing here?" I wrote to myself in my notes. Despite everything I had done to prepare, I still had woeful firsthand experience with the military. Although my father had enlisted in the navy and worked in communications with early computers for a few years in the 1960s before I was born, it was my first time as an adult on a functioning military base. If I had been ten years younger—seventeen years old—I would have been exactly in the demographic OEMA was the most interested in reaching, for one of the principal long-term goals of the Army Game Project was to normalize the army for the average American teenager as something within youth's world of experience and possibility.

I learned quickly that Wardynski loves to talk. I was happy to let him do so as he described to me the scope of the Army Game Project, which was a good deal larger than I had imagined. The original *America's Army* video game from 2002 was the sole product of the Army Game Project for many years, but in 2006 the project was dramatically expanding. After several years of success with the online game, he told me, other government entities began to approach OEMA with requests for training programs. One of the first to do so was the U.S. Secret Service, which requested a tailored version of the game for simulating training exercises for protective detail teams, tactical response units, and counter-surveillance units.

As more requests began coming in from government and military organizations, the Army Game Project decided that a separate office was necessary to handle them. The year 2006 was a period of transition as a large portion of the project management was being funneled toward Redstone Arsenal's Software Engineering Directorate (SED) near Huntsville, Alabama. Large public outreach programs such as the *America's Army* Real Heroes and the Virtual Army Experience (see chapters 4 and 5) were just getting under way as well. Ubisoft's Xbox video game, *America's Army: Rise of a Soldier*, was out in the commercial market. Most of these projects, Wardynski explained to me, were being developed by other entities that had little direct affiliation with the online video game and original version of *America's Army*.

After Wardynski had described to me all of these institutional connections that composed the Army Game Project, and asked me a few pointed questions about my own project, this first visit to West Point ended abruptly with Wardynski giving me his approval from the top to undertake ethnographic fieldwork at places central to the project. His reasons for allowing me to do so were unclear at the time; my project of "studying up" the networks of institutional power (Nader 1972), I thought, would be perceived as a nuisance at best and a threat at worst. I came to understand more about his reasons for allowing me access through subsequent conversations and encounters with him during my years of fieldwork as my travels took me to locations in the San Francisco Bay Area, Los Angeles, Huntsville, Philadelphia, Seattle, Indianapolis, and eventually back to West Point.

Although Wardynski told me then that, in his words, I had "the green light" to do my research, I still faced the challenge of gaining access to the network and figuring out which institutions were amenable and available in the first place. I was only able to do so in a more structured way two years later, after I secured research funding from the U.S. National Science Foundation, a factor that significantly helped legitimize my project to U.S. government and military personnel at West Point's OEMA, the SED in Huntsville, and elsewhere. Rather than having a single story of "arrival" at my field site, I was arriving continuously at new locations—some of which would become more receptive and familiar than others over the course of months and years. My access to these sites—development offices, marketing agencies, army bases, prerelease versions of *America's Army*, email lists, recruiting and outreach events, press briefings, specialty beer tastings—and to the people within them was a continuously negotiated process of sending emails, dropping names, obtaining permissions and passwords, making calls, and listening with a sympathetic ear to the nontrivial work-related issues of video game developers and military veterans. Wardynski had granted me the go-ahead to contact *America's Army* institutions on this first visit to West Point, but it was by no means a golden ticket.

A World of Binaries

I came to this investigation for personal reasons, but I began with a broader starting supposition that media products like video games are cultural expressions that illuminate and shape social norms and conventions. Games can signify and shape multiple ideas, worldviews, and ideologies, depending on the context in which they appear. The Army Game Project, which seeks to impose a very specific institutional message upon its game, nevertheless cannot change the fact that media are always received by a range of individuals and open to a variety of interpretations. To look at *America's Army* as a cultural product and actor in this way necessitates a broad perspective on cultural and social trends that goes well beyond taking into account the qualities of the game itself.

One major cultural trend over the past two decades has been the rising popularity and use of video games, to the point at which their use is pervasive across many populations, devices, and geographical areas. When I grew up in the 1980s video games were typically relegated to the domain of preteen boys, and the medium was commonly considered an adolescent toy. Games were portrayed in popular news media as being a dangerous medium responsible for a list of complex social issues, such as youth aggression and a decay in critical thinking. This way of thinking persists still, and consistently recurs in news media after unfortunate, publicly violent events.

Rates of violent crime consistently fell in the United States between 1994 and 2014, even as digital games came into their own as an industry (Saad 2013; FBI 2015). Research has shown that, while people might be almost imperceptibly more aggressive after playing competitive games (regardless of whether acts of violence are simulated in them), there are very inconclusive results in regards to any sort of correlation between video games and actual violence (Kowert and Quandt 2016; Schreier 2013). Paradoxically, despite the power that misguided critics still often attribute to video games as root causes of social problems, it was not until recently that mainstream American culture came to consider the medium as anything but a toy.

Games, however, have grown up alongside their players as a medium of information, entertainment, communication, and marketing. In 2015 the average age of a video game player was thirty-five years old, and 74 percent of all video game players were over the age of eighteen. Now 44 percent of gamers are women (ESA 2015), although in military-themed FPS games like *America's Army* and certain other genres of games women represent a significantly lower number of players. In addition to hostile gaming cultures of misogyny, another possible cause for the decreased participation by women in certain game genres is the persistent recycling of hypermasculine heroic narratives, which is often achieved at the expense of the character development of women figures in games (Sarkeesian 2013). This certainly applies to *America's Army 3*, as the only women depicted in the game are television news anchors, shown in a very brief nonanimated cut scene near the beginning of the game. With the transition to opening every job in the U.S. armed forces to women by 2016, including combat positions, it will be interesting to see if military-themed games come to represent this change through an inclusion of women as soldiers beyond stereotypical medic/healer roles.

These issues are important to consider as games are quickly becoming a dominant entertainment form across the American and global media landscape. Even immediately after the severe economic downturn beginning in 2008, game sales increased as the demand for them grew (Snider 2009). New mobile gaming technology supported through increasingly pervasive consumer use of phones and tablets spurred the industry through the recession and recovering economy, even as computer and console game sales decreased. Average consumers likewise embraced these mobile game apps, as they were readily networked into cell phones, were relatively inexpensive, and involved games that could be played intermittently without large time commitments. Largely due to mobile app development, game industry sales peaked in 2010 at $17.1 billion, $7 billion of which were mobile games. Reports peg recent annual industry sales at $15.4 billion, $9 billion of which were mobile game sales (ESA 2014). Compared with $2.6 billion total sales across all platforms in 1996 (ESA 2008, 11), these most recent industry figures signpost just how drastically the interactive entertainment industry has grown.

The sheer variety of video games has grown as well, and although the plots and premises of many games are inane or infused with niche interests, there are an increasing number of games on the market that present narratives and situations compelling enough to give one pause. Like film, it is a medium that is constantly reinventing itself through the creation of new genres, catering to an increasingly broader range of users. Everywhere a convergence is taking place between networked and traditional media, and games are at the center of this process. More and more, games and "gamified" systems—those that rely on game-like elements to motivate people to do certain things—influence shopping habits, communication channels between friends and coworkers, corporate arrangements of work and play, and incentive structures for undertaking difficult tasks or deterring undesirable acts. Through these channels digital games are challenging and changing the ways in which people think about and interact with the world. Games are remixing and blending categories that were once in opposition; nevertheless, in several ways we still seem caught in a world of binaries.

THE VIRTUAL AND THE REAL

The world seems often to be defined in terms of binary opposites. Good/evil, male/female, rich/poor, white/black, and chosen/heathen: binaries categorize the world and pervade much of Western thought. This way of thinking tends to produce hierarchies of violence, especially in cases involving gender, race, class, and religion, in which binary thinking ends up limiting or obscuring possible solutions to complex phenomena by defining the "other" as that which one is not. There is more to the world than binaries, but language has limited how we understand it.

Such is the case, too, with games. Digital games engender discussions on what is "real," and what happens in gaming contexts tends to be termed in common phrasings as being the opposite of "real life." Talking about "real life" as being "not-game" is something that even die-hard gamers do in everyday speech, but this kind of phrasing is disingenuous. No matter how escapist one's approach to games may be, game stimuli still bring about very real physiological and emotional responses within us. The original team of *America's Army* developers understood these factors and published research on how properly integrated sound in particular brings about these kinds of responses in digital games (Shilling, Wardynski, and Zyda 2002). Massively multiplayer online games (MMOGs) and worlds call out the false dichotomy of the virtual and the real to an even greater extent, as fully fleshed emergent economies, cultures, languages, and identities take shape through online virtual worlds.

There is a co-evolution taking place between these virtual contexts and the world of "meatspace," a term originating in cyberpunk fiction, which refers to the physical world of flesh and blood. Technologies that employ augmented reality—such as mobile devices and televisual sports-casting aids—encompass both the virtual and the actual, and much of the world's population is moving toward a reality that is increasingly mediated by both. In other ways beyond the virtual/real divide, binary configurations break down and become less distinct through militarized gaming and parallel trends. Three other distinctions that are applicable to the focus of this book are those commonly made between war and game, soldier and civilian, and work and play. The assumed stark divisions in each pair are problematic.

WAR AND GAME

On several occasions in 2009 angry protesters from Veterans for Peace, United for Peace and Justice, and other local allied groups jammed the interior of the far end of the Franklin Mills Shopping Mall in Philadelphia in front of the Army Experience Center, chanting the slogan "War is not a game!" Their rage was palpable and stemmed from (what they saw to be) the trivialization of war by the army through its use of (what they saw to be) an inherently trivial and toy-like game medium being used for military recruitment. And yet war is progressively becoming like a game, both in the ways in which it is consumed as an entertainment product and the ways in which it is fought.

This connection between war and game is not new: as liminal spaces separated from mundane, routine existence, both war and game traditionally have rituals and rules that circumscribe the space and time of each. While both have purported "rules" that may seem objective to the casual observer, the ways in which those rules are followed and enforced are inherently culture-bound. Boot camp and deployments act as resocializing mechanisms that prepare soldiers mentally to enter into a new kind of war space in which killing other humans is acceptable and sanctioned. "Magic circles" of games likewise set apart the game setting as something in which norms of social interaction apply differently, where game rules shape and cordon off the game experience as being something that is more of a ritualistic, liminal space betwixt and between everyday existence (Huizinga 1950; Turner 1967). Though they may be difficult to define, the space and time of both war and game are relegated to the atypical.

In addition to these anthropological connections between war and game are increasingly stronger socioeconomic ones. The rising variability, variety, and interoperability in games over the course of the last twenty years has coincided with the rising and essentially pervasive scale of everyday consumer interactions with visual representations and simulations of war in the United States. War games are floating signifiers that can be endlessly interpreted, even by their developers. "The military," writes media scholar Henry Jenkins (2003), "uses games to recruit and train soldiers; the antiwar movement uses games to express the futility of the current conflict; the pro-war movement uses games to express its anger against the terrorists; the news media use games to explain military strategy; and the commercial games industry wants to test the waters to see if we are going to play war games the same way other generations watched war movies." This ambiguity of meaning, when coupled with the situational gravitas of conflict, gives war games a powerful but often nonspecific emotional tenor. This is precisely what makes them so gripping to a variety of people and why video games have become a central touchstone for the way in which people now conceptualize war.

War has always been a function of vision and vice versa; the technologies of seeing have always been directly related to the technologies of fighting (Virilio 1989), and this holds true for video games. Imagining war as a video game first entered into widespread public consciousness during the 1991 First Gulf War, hailed at the time as being the "video game war" (and "Nintendo war") due to the news media's prominent and unprecedented reliance on video images of aerial bombing and digital representations of the conflict. These new gamelike properties of the war's news coverage produced an unexpected and even alarming level of detachment between the actual killing and the clean way in which it was represented. The cycle of information first experienced in the First Gulf War, in which military personnel relied on news media outside Iraq to provide them with up-to-date coverage of events inside Iraq, created a scenario that became far removed from the actual fighting. Contemporary real-time, twenty-four-hour news coverage has since perpetuated this culture of simulation in which news of an event often precedes the actual event, therefore shaping and affecting its outcome (Baudrillard 1995; Stahl 2007).

Games do have a strategic military purpose, but for most the purpose of war gaming is military entertainment—"militainment," as communications scholar Roger Stahl terms it (2007, 2010). Games do not merely reflect the realities of war, but actively shape both war and our expectations of it, even for those of us who do not play war-themed games. For those who do play, war games enable individuals to imagine themselves and role-play as soldiers in virtual contexts. This development has direct consequences in another categorical binary, that between the soldier and the civilian. The merging of war and game muddles the boundaries between the military and the nonmilitary and confounds the distinctions between soldier and civilian.

SOLDIER AND CIVILIAN

War is a problematic notion, and its limits are difficult to delineate. When is it? Where is it? Who are its participants? These questions, if approached thoroughly and thoughtfully, lead to unsettling answers that go beyond the battlefield and into the living room and the bedroom. Even though 90 percent of war casualties are noncombatant civilians, soldiers who are men dominate the popular imagery of war. The tacit boundaries between war and "not war" do not take into account the ways in which other forms of violence increase during times of war, especially among families of enlisted soldiers, which experience higher rates of domestic violence (Nordstrom 1998, 149–50). In times of deployment the strain on families with loved ones as soldiers is apparent, but issues often persist during post-deployment periods. For many veterans and their families war continues in frequently unacknowledged trauma and memories. The extent to which war affects civilians and soldiers alike in violent and traumatic ways cannot be understated and is a legacy of war that undermines the easy binary between soldier and civilian, as well as that between battlefront and home front.

War is not an "eruption" of violence due to some primal, animalistic impulses, but is a phenomenon shaped to a great degree by practices and understandings that are nonmilitary in origin (Hoffman 2011; Nordstrom 2004, 2007). War and political violence are not the "breaking down" of society but rather express and produce social realities; to consider military violence holistically and contextually means examining the systems that give it meaning and enable its production and perpetuation—systems such as government institutions, funding mechanisms, political economies, ideological frameworks, class and labor arrangements, education and recruitment initiatives, globalized networks, communication and entertainment media, structural racism and other forms of structured inequalities, and gendered behavior, which are among some of the main areas through which war operates. The processes of war shape, and are shaped by, all of these (Lutz 2006).

The upshot is that war is not limited to the domain of the soldier, nor has it ever been. War is not limited to a specific place or time; in the contemporary world it is pervasive and is something for which contemporary states are always preparing (Virilio and Lotringer 1983). Although a civil/military distinction exists, it is largely an artifice maintained through institutional and media communications. This illusory separation between the world of the civilian and that of the soldier, however, has become increasingly vague through the variety of entertainment media depictions of war, as well as the increasing cooperation between the entertainment and military defense industries over the past twenty years (Halter 2006; Lenoir 2000, 2003; Turse 2008). As a video game that touts one of its goals as "compet[ing] in the electronic entertainment space for youth mind share" (Wardynski 2009, 15) in order to encourage the consideration of military enlistment at an early age, *America's Army* actively and effectively perpetuates this ambiguity between soldier and civilian—more so than any other form of military recruitment or media campaign.

Contextualizing war means understanding that soldiers and civilians alike perform the labor of war. Like civilian jobs soldiering can become a career, a temporary employment situation, or part-time work. In making this parallel I want to be clear that I am not claiming that soldiers and civilians are essentially the same. The violence that underlies all soldiering work should not be diminished or trivialized as an aspect that sets soldiering apart from most other jobs, excepting police work and other forms of private or government security work. Nevertheless the aura of "selfless service" and patriotism that surrounds soldiering in the United States masks the ways in which it is primarily a job to which individuals regularly turn for largely financial reasons.

Civilians, more often than soldiers, are the primary casualties in war, and the lines between home front and battlefront become unclear in myriad ways. Soldiers return home from overseas with unseen injuries. Remotely piloted drones, flown over Afghanistan, Yemen, and Pakistan from bases in Nevada and North Dakota, become the new mechanism of air war. Entertainment media interpellate—or call on—individuals to imagine themselves as soldiers, and civilian labor regularly supports the industry of war. War clearly requires a lot of work and takes its toll on both civilians and soldiers, but it also involves a fair amount of play. In this sense the labor of making war in the twenty-first century is in perfect alignment with other forms of work.

WORK AND PLAY

A friend of mine who was a guild leader for the popular MMOG *World of Warcraft* once told me that the reason she stopped playing was that her play responsibilities for managing a group of over forty people were "becoming too much like work." This fairly typical experience mirrors the corporate adoption of the "play-at-work" mantra (and its darker double, the imperative to "work-at-play"), which seems not to be abating, particularly in the tech industries. Evolving technologies and techniques aimed at producing employee efficiency while mitigating burnout problematize the work-play binary, as employees continue to use networked technologies during work while extending working hours beyond discrete activities and bounded segments of time, thanks to essentially pervasive smart phones and tablets. High-tech companies like Google exemplify the corporate approach to incorporating more of an employee's life into the work environment, with flex-time "work from home" perks, legendary cafeterias, and "relaxed and casual, even whimsical" building designs (Goldberger 2013).

Work invades nonwork time through new media technologies, and the creative output of media and software industry laborers, including game developers, tends to become completely intertwined with their work. In contrast to previous eras, there is something very different going on here in regards to the way individuals working in the knowledge economy conceptualize their labor. These kinds of high-tech workers tend to consider their work as a personal endeavor of creativity, self-expression, and achievement, in direct contrast to the classic industrial salaried laborer, working eight hours a day in a factory to perform repetitive tasks that produce uniform products (Berardi 2009b, 76–77).

Although most obvious in the technology sector, the mentalities of "play *as* work" and "play *at* work" are not confined to those working as employees in the high-tech software industry, but extend to other labor sectors as well as to users of entertainment and social media technologies. Facebook's economy of likes, updates, and friends is a classic example of what media theorist Tiziana Terranova calls "free labor" wherein "productive activities . . . are pleasurably embraced [by users] and at the same time shamelessly exploited [by companies]" (2000, 37). In the current era of "big data," free downloadable apps and technology are rarely purely free, since end-user agreements typically involve the sharing of personal use information that becomes aggregated and sold to the highest bidder, with the goal of better positioning products in online spaces that are most likely to reach target markets. Free user labor is likewise harnessed by game developers through game modification tools that enable players and users to create and share their own additions to published game content beyond the original "vanilla" game. In this way game developers, publishers, and distributors maintain interest in their product and encourage the growth of creative, emergent communities that add value to their software at little or no cost.

Those who voluntarily labor without pay regularly undertake aspects of digital game development work; quality assurance "beta testing" is a prime example. Game developers sometimes discursively position this established practice of testing software prior to its release for the purpose of detecting bugs and glitches as being a reward in itself, which gives volunteer testers an opportunity to have a sneak peek at a new game. Crowdfunded beta testing work, wherein the player actually pays the company for the privilege of contributing to the game's development process prior to its commercial release, is becoming a new normal in game development. For those quality assurance game testers who are actually paid employees of a company, a state of labor precariousness due to characteristically short-term and low-wage contract work is common. For games especially, work and play quite often look the same.

The list of examples above points toward just how problematic the binary formulas of virtual and real, war and game, soldier and civilian, and work and play can be. They may have worked in the past as useful ways of describing and giving meaning to social phenomena, and they still attempt to describe aspects of the social. The result, however, is a misleading and mostly unintentional concealment of actual processes that belie the binaries.

The Militarization of Immaterial Labor

At the heart of the false dichotomies described above is an institutional force that has worked to solidify the apparent boundaries between them. By "institutions," I refer to classical disciplinary institutions, such as schools, prisons, hospitals and mental institutions, universities, governments, factories and corporations—and the military. These institutions have been most prominently examined in the work of French theorist Michel Foucault, whose work details how the eighteenth century marked a dramatic rise in various scientific and pseudoscientific techniques for controlling individual bodies and actions at the level of large populations. During this period institutional and academic disciplines developed quickly, and once they could track and monitor populations their analysis brought about new social "problems," such as birthrate, public health, military manpower, homelessness, and immigration.

The work of institutions historically has been to enforce conformity to institutionally defined norms and expectations. Institutions, at their core, wield power and discipline, either through overt coercion or subtle encouragement. This is most visible in those institutional configurations that most regularly use physical violence as means of enforcing conformity, such as prison systems and militaries, but just as true for those institutions that structure behavior through typically less overt means. It is important to note that institutions *produce* behavior by structuring actions (through physical infrastructure and architecture) and ways of thinking (through diverse messaging and instruction systems). Institutions define roles (student, mental patient, prisoner, soldier, juror, parishioner, homeless person, employee, spouse, social worker) and set boundaries; they work to delimit and solidify the differences between things, and this is the case with the binaries explored above.

Institutions regulate human populations by deploying analytical tools, including demographics, policies, laws, social systems, and (now) tools to leverage "big data." Rather than approaching individuals as merely legal or political subjects, this institutional approach regards them as living beings whose physical health, mental condition, sexuality, genetics, ability to reproduce, capability to fight, potential to work, and all other biologically related functions (the list can go on) are central to governance and supervision. While institutions are the defining structures through which power is wielded in the contemporary world, forms of power change over time and morph according to socioeconomic and political conditions. It is important to note that institutional power is not stagnant, but instead is constantly evolving, seeking out new forms of control by insinuating itself into the fabric of social life, individual behaviors, and subjectivities.[5]

One such important evolution involves the disaggregation and diffusion of institutions over the past forty years, particularly in the United States. In some cases this process has been marked by perpetual crisis, and yet the control wielded by institutions is not fading away but is instead becoming dispersed beyond the institutions themselves, expanding via globalized capital and systems of technology ever further into human biology and subjectivity (Hardt and Negri 2000, 2004). Political theorist Giorgio Agamben formulates such crises as being "states of exception" that have become an unexceptional new norm of governance (2005), and activist scholar Naomi Klein's *The Shock Doctrine* (2008) details the ways in which perpetually recurring human-made or human-exacerbated crises have intensified inequalities and been exploited for political and economic gain in the early twenty-first century.

In their own ways both Agamben and Klein are describing the evolution of institutional power into what Gilles Deleuze calls a *society of control* (1992), which is achieved when all-encompassing institutions are no longer required to produce docile subjects. Deleuze writes that "in the disciplinary societies" first described by Foucault, "one was always starting again (from school to the barracks, from the barracks to the factory), while in the societies of control one is never finished with anything—the corporation, the educational system, the armed services being metastable states coexisting in one and the same modulation, like a universal system of deformation" (1992, 5). While the domain of the military in the United States, for example, was once mostly confined to the world of the soldier, weapons, and barracks, military power in the society of control gradually becomes diffused across multiple formats, moving into schools and education systems, forms of entertainment, policing and immigration strategies, and international diplomatic efforts. For example, the California prison system, which persists as one of the most expansive and expensive in the world, is in a state of enormous financial, social, and legal crisis (Gilmore 2007; *LA Times* Editorial Board 2013). Public space becomes militarized through urban planning and policing (Davis 1990), and this has become increasingly obvious as issues surrounding police militarization and institutionalized racism have taken national center stage, beginning with events in Ferguson, Missouri, in August 2014 (Greenwald 2014).

Just as the specific power of institutions becomes more generalized, in the society of control the binary categories explored above, which were once integral to institutional power, now become blurred. The blurring of these binaries, which have to a great extent been established by institutions, is one symptom of the evolution from a disciplinary power based at the institutions to a disciplinary power diffused and distributed throughout the control society. (It is worth pointing out here that in describing this diffusionary process, I am not bemoaning the demise of the fabled "good ol' days" when we knew the differences between work and play, feminine and masculine, soldier and civilian, gay and straight, sane and insane, war and game, black and white, and so forth.)

This discussion on the ways in which institutions wield power in the early twenty-first century is highly relevant, given that *America's Army* is a game funded and produced by one of the classical disciplinary institutions—the military—but distributed through digital media networks that have become essentially pervasive in the United States. Like other total institutions the U.S. military still directs much of its disciplinary power toward persuasive and more classically authoritarian messaging formats. The products of the Army Game Project deliberately use persuasive elements as a strategy; a favorite book of the project's long-time director, Colonel Casey Wardynski, is *Persuasive Technology: Using Computers to Change What We Think and Do* (Fogg 2003). Although I hesitate to call *America's Army* "propaganda," since its approach to messaging is more sophisticated than the unidirectional mass media model of propaganda from the early and mid-twentieth century described by Herman and Chomsky (2002 [1988]), the game is still in that rhetorical tradition of persuasion through media, directed at citizens by elements of the state. Wardynski himself unapologetically considers the game as part of a continuum stemming from the Uncle Sam "I Want You" ads of World War I and propaganda movies of World War II (Chaplin and Ruby 2005, 219). The situation of *America's Army* within a militarized culture industry and economy, however, speaks to a larger, omnipresent form of military power, which is distributed more broadly across the society of control. This is the process of pervasive cultural militarization, enacted in part through the harnessing of high-tech labor and the intermeshing of the technologies and economies of entertainment and war.

As the divide between work and play breaks down, "playbor" has become a new norm, especially in the high-tech industry. This development is indicative of the stark differences between what is known as traditional Fordist and post-Fordist systems of labor, both of which draw their name from Henry Ford's model of an industrial system of automotive production. At its height during the 1940s and '50s, Fordism's general characteristics came to include factory assembly line work, unionized lifelong employment at a living wage, and the standardization of products. Although Fordist examples continue to exist, beginning in the 1970s this model gradually gave way to what has been termed "post-Fordism"—or, more broadly, post-industrialism.

As is the case with other institutions, the institution of the workplace is less discrete under the post-Fordist model. Several characteristics make it so, and these most prominently include 1) the economic privatization and deregulation of formerly state-run industries and social service programs; 2) shorter production cycles; 3) more networked and less hierarchical structures of organization; 4) greater mobility of jobs, coupled with increased instability in long-term employment and the decreased power of labor unions; and 5) the centrality of new technologies in all of these processes (Hardt and Negri 2000; Virno 2004; Weeks 2011). Among the starkest characteristics of post-Fordism is the increase in the previously discussed ambiguity between work time and leisure time. This lack of distinction regularly happens through the connectivity brought about by new forms of communication, such as mobile phones and networked devices.

Once the separation between work and nonwork time becomes ambiguous, employers privilege other qualities of human labor. While the ability to carry out manual tasks has remained essential, other skill sets have grown in importance. Like the Industrial Revolution, which brought about new industrial changes in society beyond simply factory work, new post-Fordist changes exert influence in broader contexts and require social and working relationships to depend on the exchange of information in more affective and communicative ways. Although specific types of labor have always compelled or required employees to project an intuitive and emotional tenor in their work (e.g., flight attendants, service work), post-Fordist labor more extensively capitalizes on the affective, cognitive, communicative, and social qualities of employees. Technology is a pillar post-Fordist work, which typically takes place in front of computer screens and produces intangible products. The term for the kind of work that takes place under the conditions of post-Fordist employment is *immaterial labor* (Lazzarato 1996).

Autonomist Marxist scholar Bifo Berardi refers to the individuals working under this state of affairs as members of the "cognitariat" (2009a, 2009b). This term draws on the Marxist concept of the proletariat as a class of revolutionary potential, but signals the autonomist Marxist idea that, with the disintegration of unions and labor from the 1970s onward, the primary possibilities for social change now lie in a new rising class of immaterial laborers. As a rising part of the contemporary global information and entertainment culture industry, digital games are an exemplary industry of post-Fordist immaterial labor, which is undertaken by the cognitariat (Dyer-Witheford and de Peuter 2005).

Immaterial labor privileges "soft skills" for work in areas such as video game design, and this is also a central rationalization for the army in using "soft sell" marketing and recruiting tactics through initiatives such as *America's Army*. With *America's Army*, drawing on immaterial labor is both a means—through the development and use of game technology—and an end for the army, since the privileged qualities of immaterial workers are precisely those qualities in soldiers that the army seeks to recruit through novel initiatives like *America's Army* (Wardynski et al. 2009). It is not coincidental that, historically, post-Fordist configurations not only map closely onto the diffusion and smoothing of institutional power that is the main characteristic of the control society, but also correspond to ongoing processes of militarization.

Militarization happens through industrial practices, infrastructural arrangements, policy planning, political decisions, consumer marketing, and entertainment media that have come to have vested interests in the continuation of economies that are centered on, or tied closely to, the military. Feminist sociologist Cynthia Enloe describes "militarization" as being a continual cultural and economic process whereby a person, institution, or idea comes to depend on the military or militaristic ideas for their well-being or existence. Because this development is often slow and inconspicuous, militaristic expressions and presumptions tend to take on an aura of the ordinary (2000, 3). Enloe, for example, explains how even a can of soup that contains pasta-shaped space defense satellites reflects militarized ideas that have been adopted as taken-for-granted assumptions by both the producers and consumers of soup (2000, 1–35). These kinds of micro-level processes of militarization are just as important to trace as the larger social ones, as they illuminate aspects of ordinary life that are often taken for granted.

The origins of the current militarized economy of the United States can be traced to the total war orientation of industries during World War II and the war's aftermath, when rationalizations for the continuation of high levels of military spending morphed at the beginning of the Cold War toward the contestation of a perceived Soviet threat. In 1961, as he left the presidency Dwight Eisenhower signaled the dangers of what he termed the "military-industrial complex." In his now iconic farewell address Eisenhower cautioned, "In the councils of government, we must guard against the acquisition of unwarranted influence, whether sought or unsought, by the military-industrial complex. The potential for the disastrous rise of misplaced power exists and will persist. . . . Akin to, and largely responsible for the sweeping changes in our industrial-military posture, has been the technological revolution during recent decades. . . . For every old blackboard there are now hundreds of new electronic computers" (1961).

Though it is not likely that Eisenhower could have predicted the rise of video games as an entertainment medium, he understood that the future of war would be intertwined with that of the computer. Indeed, it is so intertwined that one game developer of *America's Army* understood his work directly in relation to Eisenhower's military-industrial complex, telling me that *America's Army* "is really close to what he was talking about, the military becoming commercialized. It's almost fashionable, it's really bizarre."[6]

Today organizations devoted to the continuation of the military's close relationships with various industries exist at all levels, employ a large percentage of workers, and are central to the overall economic orientation of the United States. The stretch of this economy is vast, covering most economic sectors, including entertainment, communication, food, and academia, not to mention arms manufacturing (Turse 2008). The catchphrases that writers have used to describe what now exists build on Eisenhower's phrasing and include expressions such as the "military entertainment complex," "MIME-NET" (the military industrial media entertainment network), "empire" (with a capital "E" or a lowercase "e"), or, simply, "the complex."[7] Other kinds of "complexes" have been invented to describe different militarized or hybrid institutionalized relationships, such as the "prison-industrial complex." While these terms act as sometimes useful shorthand for describing the conduct of arrangements, practices, organizations, policies, transactions, assumptions, and ideologies in a militarized economy, they also have the potential to obscure what they attempt to describe. I regularly use the term "military entertainment complex," but also note the problems in doing so. Describing any kind of "complex" as a single monolithic entity belies the constant negotiation of contracts, incorporation of new technologies, introduction of new policies, corporate buyouts and mergers, and the other dynamic interactions between multiple parties of individuals and organizations within a militarized set of relationships. Part of the project of this book is in calling out the complexities and lived realities of militarized relationships, which are ironically exactly what is circumvented in notions of military "complexes."

The military entertainment complex is one way in which the military comes to pervade everyday life in the United States, to the point where militarized entertainment, news about military operations, and the presence of the military in characteristically nonmilitary areas (such as sports events, state fairs, and shopping malls) becomes banal and even boring. Anthropologist Catherine Lutz describes this as the "military normal" (2009), which starts to take shape the more often military needs become prioritized, the more regularly the military's presence is visible, the more habitually military metaphors come to be used in everyday language, and the more frequently military themes in news and entertainment media become an unquestioned part of the status quo. The logic of the military normal is almost involuntary on the social level in the United States, and it is difficult to escape—even for anthropologists studying it.

For this reason I go further than Enloe in my conceptualization of what militarization is and how it is perpetuated, including aspects that are not exclusively top-down and originating from state, corporate, and institutional complexes. Militarization is not an exclusively one-way phenomenon, and in the contemporary post-Fordist world militarization acts in a more performative, bottom-up, and user-initiated manner. For example, while the old Uncle Sam "I want you for the U.S. Army" ads might capture the essence of top-down early twentieth-century military recruitment techniques that are unidirectional in their messaging from institution to individual, military recruitment today happens in a performative and cybernetic way that seeks to incorporate its subjects in its process. Digital games are a textbook example in that they give players the appearance of agency in determining their actions. Like the Internet, digital games and interactive media carry a liberatory promise to the user, one that is never fully fulfilled. Between the spaces of the promise and the deliverable, militarization creeps in.

I must add that ghosts of debates centering on the issue of video games vis-à-vis violence and aggression haunt this connection between militarization and video games. Although the issue of games and violence is connected in some ways to the militarization of games, I must be clear in stating that militarization through digital games is not synonymous with violence in digital games. Despite all of my personal enjoyment of simulated violence in games, I have never once felt in my gaming experiences any kind of so-called media effect that translates to me becoming a more violent individual. These real or imagined "effects" of games are important considerations, since the way in which the army *talks about* violence in digital games points toward a rhetorical maneuvering that carefully sidesteps claims that link games to physical aggression and violence. It is important to keep in mind that violence, guns, masculinity, and even seemingly divergent concepts like the ideas of peace, women's rights, or environmentalism are all things that can be (and have been) militarized or demilitarized, depending on the context (Enloe 2000).

War, media, and immaterial labor enact dynamic interconnected processes, which are constantly morphing and changing. The ultimate product of these intertwined processes is militarization, but the cultural expressions of a militarized society are continually changing. Military-themed and military-sponsored uses of media such as *America's Army* both express and perpetuate a pervasive militarization of popular culture in the United States. As such, any notion that the military sphere in the United States is confined merely to the armed services is false.

The primary argument of this book is that digital games and simulations act as channels for enlisting and militarizing immaterial labor.

This happens at all levels, and is a result of a military imagination that positions individuals as virtual soldiers—people whose labor is, or could be, militarized in some form. Virtual soldiering is not an individual choice that people are at liberty to make, but rather the result of an institution-alizing force that spreads as a pervasive element through the society of control. In this sense everyone is essentially a virtual soldier. In this book I draw on descriptive ethnographic details in order to articulate how virtual soldiering operates, connecting the sinews between indi-vidual and institutional actors of *America's Army* to the larger cultural trends in militarization, interactive entertainment, and immaterial labor.

2   The Art of Persuasion and the Science of Manpower

OEMA's charter is to build the army of the future. It's about recruiting talent, assessing talent, deploying talent, and retaining talent.

MAJ. MIKE MARTY, *America's Army* chief operations officer, personal interview

From Personnel Management to Talent Management

In my first meeting with Wardynski, described in the previous chapter, I discovered that the roots of the Army Game Project were deeply embedded in the logics of market analysis and neoliberal business principles. It was only later, in subsequent meetings, that I came to understand how profoundly the Army Game Project pushed against traditional, institutionalized understandings of how the U.S. Army recruits and conceptualizes soldiers. At the heart of this endeavor was Wardynski's Office of Economic and Manpower Analysis (OEMA), an economic and policy-focused army interdisciplinary research institution within the Department of Social Sciences at West Point. In its market-based rationalizations OEMA challenged the entrenched recruitment and technology procurement practices of the army, and in so doing made a series of institutional rivals, if not enemies, within the greater U.S. military complex. More entrenched organizations were able to outmaneuver *America's Army* in terms of funding and contract bids. In 2009, for example, the army's PEO-STRI (Program Executive Office for Simulation, Training, and Instrumentation)[1] mediated a bid by Czech software developer Bohemia Interactive Simulations for their product *Virtual Battlespace 2* to become the official army training simulation for enlisted soldiers. This contract was essentially renewed in 2013, when Bohemia Interactive Simulations again won a competitive bid to develop the official next-gen training simulation, *Virtual Battlespace 3*.

Through his zeal Wardynski created enemies and admirers—sometimes in the same person among several people with whom I communicated. He made clear his perspective that institutions like PEO-STRI were not only competitors with the Army Game Project, but also an endemic military problem. ("These nitwits at PEO-STRI hate me," he once said.) From Wardynski's standpoint the end goal of *America's Army* had always been to increase the operational efficiency and quality of recruited soldiers and decrease unnecessary expenditures and procedures. According to him larger institutionalized organizations are marked by bloated budgets, low-quality products, and wasteful practices, along with attitudes of complacency. These efficiency objectives were often overlooked in press reports and writings that sensationalized the fact that the U.S. Army game is "taxpayer-funded" (e.g., Hodes and Ruby-Sachs 2002).

OEMA's traditional work was to provide analysis and recommendations to the army for a wide range of issues by building innovative projects to study and address systemic economic problems that the army faces in its organizational structure. Wardynski, for example, describes his PhD dissertation in policy analysis as an effort to better "understand how Army stationing practices undermine household income and increase the direct cost of manning the Army."[2] Under his supervision OEMA proposed the Officer Career Incentive Program, which worked to ensure that officers could be placed in an army occupation of their choice and attend graduate school in exchange for additional years of service (Burgess 2008). Other initiatives on which OEMA worked include putting together an effective program for tracking post–Cold War nuclear weapons stocks and various studies on the demographics and interests of West Point cadets, such as how many of them play *America's Army* in relation to other college-aged adults (Chaplin and Ruby 2005, 214).

One study by OEMA, *Towards a U.S. Army Officer Corps Strategy for Success: A Proposed Human Capital Model Focused upon Talent*, argues that a "talent-focused strategy" for recruiting officers is imperative since, due to a dearth in supply of mid-career officers, "there are increasing and accelerating signs that [the] Officer Corps will be unequal to future demands unless substantive changes are made in its management" (Wardynski et al. 2009, 3). This emphasis on "talent" accentuates a military need and desire to hire a workforce that exhibits "intelligence [and] aptitudes for rapid learning and adaptation. Talented officers . . . discern quickly patterns of activity within new situations, and . . . leverage these innate aptitudes to become expert in the competencies to which they are drawn. These may range from deep technical skills to broad conceptual or intuitive abilities, all of which the Army requires" (Wardynski et al. 2009, 15). In conjunction with this published assessment Wardynski supervised the creation of a "talent management system" for officers that would place "the right leader, in the right position, at the right time."[3]

An underlying issue, however, is in "accessing, developing, and employing talented people [whose] intellectual agility allows them to master diverse competencies demanded now and in the future. Such a strategy . . . will move the Army beyond personnel management to talent management" (Wardynski et al. 2009, vi). This published study is separate from the Army Game Project, but the fact that it originated from the same institution and director underscores how the need for "talented" army laborers could be addressed, in part, through novel recruitment solutions like *America's Army*. At its core *America's Army* is an initiative for moving toward the management of talented potential soldiers, as it actively engages a demographic of young men who have access to computers and basic competencies that are most valued by the working cognitariat.

These descriptions of what constitutes a "talented" workforce coincide quite closely with the general characteristics of immaterial labor in post-Fordist knowledge economies. Like the need for officer "talent," immaterial labor tends to emphasize flexibility and adaptability, as well as affective, cognitive, and communicative forms of labor over the characteristically Fordist privileging of structured time and manual labor, epitomized by assembly line work—or, in this case, the "cog in the wheel" characterization of the grunt soldier. Computers and new technologies are central in configuring immaterial labor, and Wardynski himself had been writing about the need for the army to move toward an informational economic model of labor since at least the mid-1990s. The army's "expanding reliance on information technology," he argued, "will give rise to an increasing requirement for highly educated individuals" who will be drawn to work in growing nonmilitary high-tech sectors (1995, 61). *America's Army* actively engages a demographic of young men who have access to computers and basic knowledge of the informational competencies most valued among high-tech, immaterial laborers, and is an initiative for recruiting talented virtual soldiers/immaterial workers who might otherwise be attracted to nonmilitary high-tech work. One criticism that has been leveled at *America's Army* is that it does not provide equal access to the game for underprivileged and minority youth who may not have access to computers in their domestic life to play the PC-exclusive game. If *America's Army* is one way for OEMA to solve its projected supply problems in recruiting talented army laborers, this assessment misses the point that it is precisely the persons who have regular access to computers that *America's Army* wishes to reach.

In their analysis of the history of video games, Greig De Peuter and Nick Dyer-Witheford demonstrate how game development work, once seen in the 1970s and early 1980s as a line of flight from the institutionalized and dehumanizing structure of Fordist work, was ultimately reappropriated and co-opted by the capitalist economy as perhaps the most quintessential industry exemplifying post-Fordist immaterial labor (2009). This reappropriation continues in both military and nonmilitary spheres. Video games originated primarily from within military-funded initiatives but quickly came to be associated with a growing counterculture of antiauthoritarian hackers. It is safe to say that capital has, for the most part, tamed the rebelliousness and recaptured the labor of the knowledge economy and the cognitariat. The military, however, is still in the process of remilitarizing this form of immaterial labor. The logics enumerated by OEMA, the Army Game Project, and Wardynski himself exemplify a military desire to do just this. *America's Army* is a tool for militarizing, recruiting, managing, and ultimately recapturing the labor of the post-Fordist cognitariat.

To this end *America's Army* and OEMA implemented a variety of persuasive and rhetorical strategies to address potential political flashpoint issues, such as military recruitment and video game violence, to make the case that the game and its franchise was a legitimate use of government funds. Wardynski understood that solid, consistent messaging by the *America's Army* franchise was necessary in order to carefully navigate the murky political waters surrounding army recruitment funding, accusations of military propaganda, and video game violence. Wardynski's explanations are not only informational in showing these persuasive tactics of the Army Game Project, but are also demonstrative of his own persuasive power; his personality was so forceful that in my conversations with him I regularly felt compelled to believe his explanations indisputable, and this was a common feeling among employees working in the Army Game Project. Because Wardynski's words capture a part of the sheer persuasive faculty that he commanded and sought to infuse into the game, I relate his explanations of the Army Game Project at length below.

In the Office of Wardynski

In the heart of West Point, Wardynski and I sat down to talk in his modest office facing the Hudson River.[4] His market approach went straight to the issue of increasing demand among tech-savvy "kids" (his terminology) to join the army. In Wardynski's words, "We [at OEMA] assume that markets are pretty efficient, and we know that government isn't. So if you can make government behave more like markets, maybe you would be better off." Central to OEMA's strategy for doing so was a proposed tailoring of the army's Reserve Officers' Training Corps (ROTC) program. ROTC courses and programs in universities across the United States are one of four paths to becoming an officer in the U.S. Army. In addition to regular courses, periodic weekend training activities, and morning physical exercise, they typically involve an eight-year commitment to the army after graduation (four years' active duty and four years' inactive/reserve duty) in exchange for tuition reimbursement and a stipend while a university student. "So if we were looking to see where to put our ROTC programs," Wardynski asked, "what's the hardest thing to do in terms of getting an ROTC cadet? Is it training, or is it getting them interested in ROTC? My thinking is [that] the hardest part is getting talented people interested—building demand. So if building demand is the hard part, the question is really a function of two things: What schools do they want to go to and at those schools what could we do to make them interested in ROTC?"

ROBERTSON ALLEN: It's pretty specific to the school and the place.

CASEY WARDYNSKI: Yeah, and so given that we want crackerjack people, what schools are they interested in? Because if we're at the wrong school, we're out of luck no matter what we do. So that's a whole different question from what the army asks. Right now, the army is asking, how much do we get out of our ROTC battalions at the other campuses? Well, if you're at the wrong campuses, you're never going [to solve your underlying problems] with that analysis. You have to ask a whole different kind of question: Of the people that want to go into the military, where do they want to go to school? [. . .] So [OEMA] built the army a framework for how to deal with these questions globally. We asked, of the people who come into the army directly who have a college degree, where do they come from? And of people who are applying to West Point from all over the United States, where else did they apply? And you find out that it's really a whole different set of schools.

RA: Where are they?

CW: The Pennsylvania schools [Penn State and U Penn] are at the top of their league. And a lot of schools [that have ROTC] aren't even on the list. That's a question about markets—where does the market say we should be, versus where are we? So with game technology, the question would be that we don't really understand all the attributes of games all that well. We know there's goodness there, but we don't know what the ingredients are and in what ratios. But there are things that we do know. We know they move fast [in the market]. We know that they are extremely interesting to the same sort of people in the military—young males. For example, we created a Facebook page for the new launch of *America's Army 3* about two or three days ago. Ninety-four percent of the people who are fans of our Facebook page are male. That's pretty good information right there—we're in the right market.

RA: Two days and you already know that.

CW: Yep, I think we have about 2,600 fans now; 94 percent are male, 30 percent are thirteen to seventeen, 21 percent are eighteen to twenty-four, and 23 percent are twenty-five to thirty-four. The vast majority are under age thirty-four. Okay, that's good. So there's native interest there and we're in the right spot for this game technology thing. And the kind of game we're making, it's not Chutes and Ladders, it's a first-person [shooter] game. So that's how you narrow in the genre. And the next thing to ask is what you can get from this game. They evolve very quickly and are pretty much at the cutting edge all the time. The industry is over there, moving at light speed— better, faster, quicker, more players, more immersion, more intuitive. All of these are the attributes of good games, and when you look at the army, where are we going? We run on [game] engines that nobody has ever even heard of. We run on engines that were economic failures.

Here Wardynski refers to the fact that *America's Army* uses versions of the commercially successful Unreal Engine, which is a familiar game development tool among industry game developers. Other outsourced military games and simulations, such as the official army simulation trainer vbs2 (now vbs3), run on less common game engines with which commercial game developers typically are not as familiar. The politics of game-engine choice was an important aspect of how *America's Army* positioned itself in terms of its competitors and audience. By drawing on established game-design conventions and technology in the commercial fps market, oema sought to tap into the array of other hugely successful military-themed combat games in the commercial market. For example commercial sales for *Call of Duty: Modern Warfare II* (2009), released the same year as *America's Army 3*, were over $310 million in its first week of sales in the United States and United Kingdom, making it the most successful release for any form of entertainment media ever at that time. By mid-January 2010 the game had grossed over $1 billion in revenue (Cork 2009; bbc News 2010). But while commercial military games sought to gain a market share among the target demographic of teenage to thirty-something males, the purpose of *America's Army* hinged on gaining headway within a separate market—that of the market for "talented" future military recruits.

Because the target demographic for both of these markets was essentially the same, creating a video game developed and produced by the U.S. Army was a logical opportunity to leverage a preexisting market demand for military games by co-opting messages about the army that were already in circulation in the electronic entertainment industry. This is easier said than done, and the ability of *America's Army* to tap into "native demand" was the major aspect that differentiated the game from other military uses of games for recruitment. Wardynski told me:

CW: There have been a lot of efforts to mimic [*America's Army*] that haven't succeeded, which points to the fact that this isn't easy. Now, many of those efforts were doomed from design; they hadn't thought through the key ingredients: is there native demand?[5] We didn't have to create demand; it was already there. So the navy gets it in their head to have a game [*Strike and Retrieve* (U.S. Navy 2005)] but where's the native demand for things that look like the navy in a game? There's very little demand [for] a submarine game or an airplane game that involves being a pilot or a commander. Do they hire for those jobs? No. So how do you make the jobs the navy is hiring for be interesting in games? Well, it doesn't seem like anybody has been able to figure it out yet. Is it likely that the military is going to figure it out if the game industry can't figure it out? No. So what do they [the U.S. Navy] come up with? A fish game. All the ten people who have played it have discovered [that], but the navy can check the logs that they have a game. Is there an air force game? Not really. Do they need one? Probably not. Is there evidence of existing demand? Pretty thin. *Microsoft Flight Simulator . . .*

RA: It's an older crowd of people who play flight simulators.

CW: Exactly, so even if there is demand, is it the demand [that they want]? They're in the wrong part of the curve. The next question would be, if you're going to do it, do you have the wherewithal to do it right? Because if you do it wrong, there's no point in doing it. There are enough alternatives for kids with games that just because your game is free doesn't mean that the kid is going to come play it. So if you don't do a high-quality product, in my mind you might as well not do anything because you are probably going to end up hurting yourself more that helping yourself. The fact that we could do a top-quality product, being that we are in the government, to me is very surprising. Which is unfortunate, but it's because of our procurement systems. They move at dead slow speed [and are] optimized for doing business with very large companies that have a high threshold for pain in terms of being paid late and having lots of rules and regulations.

RA: How difficult is it to operate as if there is a market within an organization that doesn't see it that way?

CW: It's hard, because we're constrained by government procurement and contract rules. We're constrained by governmental thought processes, which see a year as fast or two years as fast; whereas in the game industry a year or two years is pretty slow. So the frame of reference is entirely different. That cultural shift is really tough. And the word "game" is involved. For the first seven years [I was doing *America's Army*], using the word "game" meant "toy," which is kind of crazy because the army invented war games.

Wardynski frames the differences between U.S. military/government procurement practices and game development industry practices as being largely *cultural*. It is telling, though, that while the California-based game developers of *America's Army* viewed OEMA as an arm of bureaucratic government—the symbolic antithesis of game development and at the top of the feudal hierarchy in which they described themselves working—Wardynski worked to position OEMA as a vocal challenger to institutionalized government procedures, such as established conventions of recruiting. He hoped to leverage the persuasive abilities of games to enable "kids" to start thinking about the army not as a fallback option but as a first choice for a future career. Doing so required an entirely different approach to recruiting from typical army methods.

CW: The key idea of *America's Army* was that there was a market failure that was hurting the army's ability to recruit kids. Part of it is because of the recruiters, part of it is because of the army, and part of it is because of the way kids receive and process information about the army. And the things that the army has been doing demand no proof that they should continue being done. For example, there's no question that we need recruiters. Nobody ever asks that question. Well, I question it; I'm not sure we need recruiters. I don't understand why we need a military guy to go recruit a kid to be in the military. You don't have an IBM guy go out and recruit a kid to work at IBM; you have headhunters and people to go to college fairs who know IBM. You might have a few recruiters, but really they are human-resource people who are more in the screening role than the recruiting role. Now, I can see the army having screeners to verify that these kids would be a good match, just like IBM would do, but we have reverse-screeners: instead of trying to keep out the bad fits, we're trying to force everyone in that could possibly fit and then trying to see if we could get them to be a good fit after the fact. Well, in World War II that might have made sense, but in the information age it doesn't. We don't need that many kids, really, and the kids that we do need we want them to be a good fit because they are volunteers. If they're not a good fit, they are going to cost a fortune, they are going to be unhappy, and it doesn't fit well with the market model. So I question the fact that we need recruiters. Could we do it virtually by getting kids interested in the army, by test-driving, by virtually being a part of it? By having them visit bases, do Junior ROTC? I think we can do a lot more of that, but the fact that we need recruiters is not questioned.

RA: How is that received by army recruitment?

CW: Not well. It's slow to adapt because it's a risk-adverse business. And I can understand that because if they miss their objectives, they're the ones who are going to be in the hot seat. It's hard to crack that nut. It grows its own feedstock, so recruiters who like it stay and become recruiter-recruiters. That process that they grew up in is a process that they believe in and are going to perpetuate.

RA: It becomes completely institutionalized.

CW: Completely institutionalized, whether it fits the circumstances anymore or not. So the army does recruiting events [. . .] and the army will have a report about how many "events" they did this weekend and what they got. I'll be like, well okay, [*America's Army*] had one hundred thousand events this weekend, because every mission in *America's Army* is an "event." They are just virtual, and they cost us a nickel. People forget that "return on investment" (ROI) has a numerator and a denominator. They always think of the numerator as fixed and the denominator as fixed, but if you drive your cost out of the equation, now you're in a world of disruptive technology that puts the other guys out of business because it doesn't have to get you much. [We] challenge a lot of rules of thumb in the army about why we are doing business the way that we do. Is there another way to do it that is cheaper and gets the same effects? Or a way that is cheaper and gets lower effects, but when you do the math you're still farther ahead? Or a way that is cheaper and gets you better effects?

RA: Has that been the rationale around the project since its inception?

CW: Right, that the costs are so fundamentally different. *America's Army* costs $4 million a year to build, and hosting online is about another $2.5 million, and the rest is whatever you want to do with it for marketing and events.[6] A normal game would have $10 to $40 million [devoted to marketing], depending on the game, and it would be a big deal. We don't have that kind of money. We're virtual, so we don't need shelf space, but it would be nice to have a little money so we could be up front and center on places like Steam [store.steampowered .com] or Fileplanet [www.fileplanet.com] so that kids who aren't familiar with the product could at least see that it's there and try it for free.[7]

But we face a lot of questions, like what is the ROI for *America's Army*? Okay, we get X number of hundred million man-hours of play. So how does that equate to anything the army normally thinks about? The normal marketing model is that, first, you want to make people aware that you have a product. Awareness is measured in terms of impressions, how many people saw it. So let's say a million people saw an ad on TV: a million impressions. How long did they see it? Thirty seconds for a million people—what is that? That's about eight thousand hours of viewer time. Did they pay attention? Maybe. Maybe they use Tevo, or went to get coffee or coke. Whose attention? Is it grandma, or is it Billy who is nineteen? We don't know. What were the demographics of the TV show's viewers you ran the ad on? Well, they generally are this, but who knows. So you try and compare a million game hours of *America's Army* to that. A million hours of *America's Army* are worth a hell of a lot more because: a) they didn't Tevo it; b) it's focused attention; and c) we're way beyond the "did you know there's an army?" part. In *America's Army* you're part of the army. So we can't even have a reasonable, sane discussion about comparing *America's Army* with the number of "impressions."

"In *America's Army*, you're part of the army." This direct claim on the place of the player in *America's Army* is an unambiguous example of the military conceptualization of virtual soldiering through games. Older unidirectional models of mass media predicated on the dissemination of media from a central node to many viewers—television, film, radio—interpellate viewers in a far different manner than video games, which require participatory behavior and, to varying degrees depending on the game in question, cocreation of the media experience. This element of participatory cocreation present in digital games involves users within a more interactive and engaging messaging environment, in which institutional power is better able to immerse individuals in its logics and world views. "Serious games" and "advergames" like *America's Army* have specific purposes and messages to impart, and they seek to persuade users, much like propaganda (Nieborg 2005). Classic "propaganda" in the traditional sense of the term, however, denotes a one-way messaging configuration from media producer to media consumer, and for this reason I hesitate to use the term in regards to *America's Army*, even though Wardynski himself views the game as being in the same tradition as government recruitment propaganda from previous eras. Heather Chaplin and Aaron Ruby's book *Smartbomb*, which Wardynski suggested that I read, describes him as claiming that *"America's Army* is not that unique. He says that it's just part of a continuum dating all the way back to Uncle Sam posters of World I or the propaganda movies of World War II. And he makes no apologies" (Chaplin and Ruby 2005, 219).

While *America's Army* had the same recruitment goals as "legacy" models of recruitment that employ more unidirectional messaging methods, the entrenchment of recruitment programs like the military sponsorship of NASCAR and expensive television ads during sporting events was a constant obstacle for OEMA in convincing senior government and military officials about the efficacy and legitimacy of *America's Army*. Wardynski explained:

> Part of the problem with competing with the bureaucracy and institutions is that it's hard to institutionalize. And part of the risk of becoming institutionalized is that you become part of the problem. So for senior leaders we brief, there are things called "programs of record." [. . .] They are there come fair days and bad days; they've got a budget. In the business operating mind they get a little less hungry and less lean. To draw it out on a blackboard, innovation kind of goes algorithmic—increasingly you're on the flat part of the curve. So many senior leaders aren't crazy about programs of record. *America's Army* isn't a program of record. It is funded out of the secretary of the army's recruiting initiative. It is one of his initiatives and has been since day one. It could be zeroed out at any point if it's not performing, and it can grow if it is. It is growing usually because there has always been an advocate for it at the senior level of the army. [. . .]
>
> All the literature on persuasive technology and behavioral economics supports our approach,[8] but the legacy [recruiting] system is very difficult to defeat. There are a lot of jobs, a lot of money tied up

in it. I think their budget this year for the legacy recruiting stuff was $167 million; we're in the range of $4 million. [But if] you look at where firms are putting their money into marketing, TV is not it. TV is dying, print is dying, radio is dying, and online is what's growing. Why does the army value TV so much? I have no idea. It's a one-way communication method that is extremely general in nature.

At the first principles level, I would question if anything the army is doing is right. [The army gets] away with what we do because we have an unlimited budget apparently. Or at least when we get in trouble and the country needs us, the budget pretty much becomes unlimited, right? Just because we can do that doesn't make it right. Now when the army throws those resources at it, it may succeed in the recruiting mission, but may not have done itself any long-term favors because the people that were brought in may not really have any idea of what they are doing.

Mitigating Moral Panic with a "Puff of Blood"

In the army's view commercial game developers do not get it right in several ways: Hollywood-sounding explosions, for example, are digitally faked in most other games, while three-quarters of the audio samples from *America's Army 3* were recorded on-site at locations such as firing ranges. Minute details of uniforms and gear are, likewise, sometimes inaccurate in entertainment media that portray the army, and these small details remain important to soldiers and veterans. Army rules of engagement and doctrine are often not emphasized in games and films, and entertainment media, in attempts to depict the grittiness, tragedy, or complexities of war, might try to portray soldiers as more complex figures than single-dimensional "good guys" (although there are also plenty of commercial films and games that do not try to do this). All of these are ways in which entertainment studios misrepresent the army, according to Wardynski. To use his phrasing, these kinds of media portrayals negatively contribute to "human biases in decision making" about joining the army. OEMA sought to change this kind of messaging in popular entertainment media by being very explicit about the kinds of rules soldiers are required to follow, how soldiers operate as a team, and how violence is, in theory, used as a means to an end by the military, and not as an end in itself. Wardynski told me:

> CW: The real rub is that there is always the dichotomy between entertainment and the purpose of the game. We understand that entertainment serves a role here; it's the motivating factor that draws the game into pop culture. If the game wasn't fun to play and entertaining and all of those things, nobody would play it. But the United States Army is not in the entertainment business. There is a reason that we are using entertainment as a vehicle to educate. Well, if there's no education there, there's no point [. . .] because the fundamental reason we're using entertainment is to get into pop culture and overcome these human biases in decision making to get at some of the goodness that B. J. Fogg at Stanford talks about in his work on persuasive technology.[9]
>
> The neat thing about games is that you don't have to wait five years [for the educating]. We can compress time and get to the inputs and outputs of decision making and see why the army cares about integrity. It's not because mommy said it was a good idea but because that guy's life actually depends on me knowing what the hell I'm doing. The deeper things you're trying to bring across is that there are a lot of games with guns, but there's only one army game because it isn't just guys with guns; it's guys with sanction, and that sanction has a set of expectations surrounding it which are the values. They are the army's values, but we didn't make them up. We know what America expects of us and they are a list of basic things that cordon behavior into an area of acceptability [which most Americans are] going to be pretty comfortable with. That is an army. That's the key idea that we're trying to put across.
>
> RA: In other games like *Call of Duty* . . .
>
> CW: Yeah, you don't have that. That's not their purpose. They're an entertainment tool.

RA: I heard somewhere, and I've always liked this phrase, that *America's Army* is what the army wants itself to be (Lawson et al. 2007).

CW: Yes, we're not perfect either as an army, but this is a model of how we hope we behave. It's actually a model of how we hope our recruiters think about the problem, because we got to be very frank and open and honest about the army. It doesn't do any good to hide the warts and the difficult parts from kids—the combat and all of that.

Informing Wardynski's approach to recruitment articulated here is the reality of army recruiting methods, in which promises are often made to prospective recruits about placements, jobs, and other possible benefits, which may never materialize once they sign on the dotted line. Although such tactics are employed by some recruiters to meet their recruitment quotas, they rarely benefit either the military or new recruits in the long run, and work against the very kinds of systemic issues that OEMA was attempting to redress through its initiatives. It was my impression that Wardynski felt misunderstood when public critics of *America's Army* and skeptics from government offices began querying the game's goals and methods. In his eyes they were asking the wrong kinds of questions about the game, questions shaped by: 1) criticisms of established military recruitment practices, criticisms that Wardynski shared himself; and 2) a culture of "moral panic" that conflates the playful performance of simulated game violence with actual violent crime. To illustrate, Wardynski recounted a conversation that he had with a congressional staffer three weeks prior to my interview about depictions of violence in *America's Army*. It was still fresh on his mind since it had been

a pretty pointed discussion. And at one point she said, "Nobody dies in your game." They were accusing us of glossing over that, and I told her, "Wait a minute. On one hand you're saying that the violence bothers you. And on the other hand you're saying that the glossing over of the consequences of the use of force and the fact that people get hurt [bothers you]. Well, we're not operating in a vacuum. There's a whole range of information that kids have about the army besides the army game. They know they can get blown up. They know they're going to combat and all of that. What they don't know is what it is like to be a member of one of our teams and how we operate. They don't know about the values and what they mean, really. They don't know how we get them ready. And anyway, you can get hurt in the game. You can get killed in the game." "Yeah, but there's not a lot of blood," she said. So I'm like, "Well, how much would be enough?" Kids get it. They get the drift. They know what it's like when they get in here. We're going a long way from where the army used to be with posters and TV and commercials where nobody had a gun.

It was a fine line that *America's Army* toed in regards to objective degrees and subjective interpretations of violence in video games, and this was often the most controversial element of *America's Army* and its other public recruitment campaigns like the Virtual Army Experience (VAE; see chapter 5). The army sought to mitigate these issues by purposefully following the rubric for game ratings established by the independent Entertainment Software Ratings Board (ESRB), which was created in 1994 after Congress threatened the domestic video game industry with federal regulatory oversight if it did not institute an age-appropriate ratings classification system for its products. To obtain a "Teen" rating, games such as *America's Army* should have no post-mortem manipulation of bodies, no graphic amounts of blood, and no dismemberment. *America's Army* was deliberately designed to fall within these levels appropriate to an audience of teenagers, ages thirteen and up, since it is at this age period when most individuals begin understanding and imagining their options for future careers.

By further implementing army rules of engagement (ROE) that penalized the extralegal executions of enemies who are incapacitated and secured as prisoners of war, the game pushed in-game behavior toward army-sanctioned violence. Wardynski was adamant, however, that the possibility for misusing military violence should still be available in the game as long as players were held accountable for the consequences of their actions. It is possible, for example, to shoot the obnoxious drill sergeant in basic training, but before the player can see the gruesome results of this act they are immediately placed in a prison cell in Fort Leavenworth. Disarmed and secured enemies can be killed—or "double tapped," in gamer slang—in *America's Army 3* (a popular tactic among some of the game's developers), but for this action the player loses "honor" points, which contribute to advancement and status in the game. Having several combat infractions also results in military imprisonment.

With these and other specific elements in the game design of *America's Army* and its other products like the VAE, the visual representational level of violence is significantly lower than other military-themed first-person shooters. A "puff of blood"[10] is the only visual indexing of corporal injury in the game. But over the course of its existence as a game, the aura of moral panic surrounding video games and violence has played a large part in the reception of *America's Army* by both antiwar protesters and congressional lawmakers. Recurrent media coverage that makes both causal and casual connections between video games and violent crime, despite any consistent scientific evidence, has held the medium responsible for a whole list of social ills, including addiction, depression, antisocial behavior, violence, racism, sexism, and improper parenting (Kowert and Quandt 2016; Thierer 2009).

The political import of this press coverage was made apparent to me at the California development studio, when game developers received public relations training prior to the 2009 San Francisco Game Developers Conference on how to speak about in-game violence to members of the press: "If someone asks you about the army training kids to fight and kill," the *America's Army* public relations manager directed, "just say, 'We're not here to talk about that' or 'That's not my area of expertise.' 'No comment' is not a good response." Earlier that year, a protest at the San Francisco headquarters of Ubisoft, the former publisher of console versions of *America's Army: Rise of a Soldier* (2005) and *America's Army: True Soldiers* (2007), prompted current *America's Army* game developers to change the signs outside the office building from "America's Army" to "Digital Consulting Services," a military subcontractor and their parent company.

Due to this history, Wardynski and the Army Game Project took pains to distance *America's Army* and related venues like the Virtual Army Experience from moral-panic discourses fixating on the purported effects of violent video games. The VAE, in particular, had been the target of protests at several of its tour locations at state fairs, air shows, and other large-scale public events. In their rationalizations of their objections to the VAE, protest organizations such as Veterans for Peace regularly used moral-panic discourses that vilified games as a medium and connected games to other "social ills." At one *America's Army* tournament/recruitment event, for example, a Veterans for Peace member was quoted as describing *America's Army* as being "like military pedophilia" and "giving candy to kids" (Meunier 2008).

RA: So what would you say to someone who says that the Virtual Army Experience (VAE) glorifies violence?

CW: "The army's not a game. It glorifies violence."

RA: "War is not a game."

CW: I think the way I'd approach that would be, first, why the VAE? Why not [other things like] Strength in Action Zone, or air shows, or just recruiters? I think the reason we're talking about the VAE is because it interests kids, the seventeen- to twenty-year bunch. They find it fascinating and the other stuff they couldn't be more bored by. So it's okay if the other stuff is a waste of money, but what we're doing is actually effective [at recruiting and saving money]. Now, are we glorifying war? I don't know, I'll tell you what we're doing and you figure it out. [The VAE is] a half-hour story, and who is going to write a book with no climax? What's the point of the story—the climax is usually the point. You lead up to it, you got it, and then you explain why it was important to the book. The climax of our story as a soldier is that we spend most of our lives preparing for stuff most of us hope is never going to happen, called combat. But if it does, that's the point. If there was never a chance of combat, would the United States have an army? No. They'd have a fire department or a police department, but we wouldn't have an army. We do something different. So the point of the military is combat—either preventing it, deterring it, or if worse comes to worse, fighting it. That's the climax of being a soldier. Everything we do prepares you for that so that we can do what this book here [*points to U.S. Code volumes on his bookshelf*] says we are supposed to do. Title 10, U.S. Code gives us our mission: "The U.S. Army is designed to fight and win the nation's wars on land."[11] That's our only function, according to that book. We have other jobs, but that's our function. So, you told us to do that in law, that's what we organize ourselves to do, but we're supposed to keep that a secret from the kids? That's asinine, right?

We're going to fight and win the nation's wars on land: that is the climax of the story of the U.S. Army, but we're not going to mention it. That makes no sense to me. So if we do mention it, what's the context? Is that all that you do? How do you get ready to do that, and after you come back, what do you learn from it? The reason we have a climax is that it paints the picture of why we have basic training, why it's hard, why Mommy and Daddy can't come, why we have discipline and values and teams and all that junk because when you're in combat there's no time to figure it out. Everybody's life is dependent on you knowing your job and being disciplined enough for them to count on you, not to shoot at everything on God's green earth, but just the bad guys, to watch your zone and trust that your buddy is watching his. So the climax, if you leave it out of the VAE, what's the point of everything? It's hard to tell a story about these different occupations—here's what they do and how they operate together, here's how we get them ready. And here's a guy who has really been to combat and here's how what you just saw is related to add the human touch. That's the VAE. If I'm leaving out the climax of the story to me that is disingenuous. We're not glorifying anything; we're giving you the whole damn book. You make up your own mind if you think it's glorious or not. Most of us don't think it is. It's worth doing because this country's worth defending, and there are bad people out there—a lot of 'em— that don't like our way of life. We didn't choose to go to any particular war, you sent us. When you send us, we like to be ready and we like to win, because we assume you sent us to win.

At this point, Wardynski had become so animated in his speech that it was unclear to me who the "you" was whom he was addressing. Was it me? The American people? Was it the U.S. Congress? In his next comment, though, the target of his antipathy was made clear in his return to the congressional staffer, whom he had brought up earlier:

And this woman, this damn woman, she said something about one of our Real Heroes guys [see fig. 3; see also chapter 3] as I was explaining this to her, and she said, "When your Real Hero survived that action he was in," and I [stopped her and] said, "Whoa, he didn't survive that. We don't send soldiers to the battlefield to survive. We send them to win. We send them to *dominate*. You don't send the U.S. Army in harm's way just to get by. If you send us for that, you're sending the wrong crew. So you're missing the point again. That book says that you told us to win. We're not leaving that part out. We're going organized to win." She's in the Defense Armed Services Committee and she didn't understand the first thing about why we have an army apparently.

Wardynski's discernible vitriol over such interpretations that do not conform to official army messaging frameworks led me to probe further about his thoughts regarding the then-current situation of the Army Game Project, and specifically the Virtual Army Experience. In 2009 a congressman and two-time presidential candidate from Ohio, Dennis Kucinich, proposed defunding the VAE to Congress, using the justification that "the VAE shields participants from the realities of killing while glorifying the taking of human life in a thinly veiled attempt to recruit new soldiers. Making matters worse, if a child wants to take part in the simulation, the Army collects his or her contact information, as well as an assessment of the child's performance in the simulator." Kucinich further argued that the funds for the touring simulation, which ran nearly $10 million in 2007 (significantly more than *America's Army*), could be better spent during the economic downturn (2009). Kucinich's proposal created a small media sensation, and Wardynski subsequently invited him for a tour of the VAE. "He visited for about forty-five minutes with us and seemed eminently reasonable, paid close attention, talked to all of our guys, interacted with everything that we had there. I thought it was a pretty neat experience, frankly. I was pleasantly surprised [and] on the way out [. . .] he said, 'I'd just like you to look at the age-appropriateness of it.'"

Wardynski, long experienced in handling such flashpoint issues, had anticipated this kind of remark and redirected attention and responsibility for the age-appropriateness of militarized violence in *America's Army* and the VAE back to Kucinich and the U.S. Congress. He recalled for Kucinich the 1994 agreement between Congress and the video game industry to establish the independently run ESRB for game ratings, and he noted that *America's Army* is rated "Teen." In Wardynski's words:

> I said, "Well, we did [look at the age-appropriateness of the VAE.]. In fact, we looked to Congress for guidance and we found it in the form of your agreement with the ESRB on how to rate games. We rate the VAE in the same way that the ESRB established for games. And *America's Army* serves as the underlying technology, so that's how we arrived at our conclusion. So if Congress would like to give us different guidance, we're in receive mode, but we did look at it, and we continue to look at it, and we're very careful about what we put in here."
>
> We're not using this [purely] for entertainment, but we do use entertainment as a vehicle to engage interest. The purpose is education. It's not glorification or anything else, it's education. And you're going to know after you walk out of the VAE as well as you could know it if this is something that I would want to do, or is this about as far away from anything that I would want to do as it could be? And if it is, it's served its purpose, because you know you need to do something else. That's the volunteer army. We think it's a good system. [. . .] What we are trying to do is to speak to young folks in a way that they find relevant and are comfortable with and present the army in ways that haven't been presented before and give them a far more comprehensive picture of it than you could with just commercials and posters. [. . .] We have thought this through pretty carefully—that doesn't mean we can't improve it, but we've been at it for a number of years trying to make sure what we're doing makes sense given the army's mission and our country.

As Wardynski's comments and stories show, there was persuasive work being done at multiple levels within the Army Game Project, and the future of the franchise depended on such work. (By this point in the interview, even I felt targeted and influenced by Wardynski's rhetoric and salesperson's facility for persuasion.) The game and franchise had as its primary goal the persuasion of players and users to enlist in the army or, failing that, to accept it more willingly as a legitimate, commonplace institution—part of the "military normal" of virtual soldiering (Lutz 2009).

Wardynski and OEMA, however, devoted significant work toward other persuasive efforts in other directions to sustain *America's Army*. Through his own persuasive aptitude and formidable self-styled "Godfather" disposition, Wardynski created allies when it was possible and exercised a penchant for firing employees and contractors. Convincing the U.S. government that the game and its constituent products were effective, economical, and ethical was a principally important task. As a project that received limited Department of Defense funding due to not being a "program of record," the Army Game Project did not have the institutional security afforded to more conservative army recruitment programs. Because it directly challenged the entrenched techniques of army recruitment—TV ads, sports sponsorships, events like Strength in Action Zone, and even the effectiveness of army recruiters themselves—the Army Game Project created political rivalries within the Army Recruitment Command (USAREC). In a lucrative market for military training simulations, other organizations like the U.S. Army's PEO-STRI office threatened the territorial claims that *America's Army* had initially made on military serious games. These rivalries underscore the heterogeneous nature of the "military entertainment complex" and the U.S. military in general.

Other persuasive fronts that the Army Game Project consistently fought were in disassociating the project from negative scapegoating discourses that connected video games with increased individual aggression and violent behavior. At moments there were palpable pushbacks against the game from multiple organizations and groups. The American Civil Liberties Union (ACLU), for example, wrote in a 2008 report on U.S. military recruitment practices that "by exposing children younger than seventeen to military recruitment, the United States military violates the terms of the Optional Protocol" to the Convention on the

Rights of the Child, which was ratified by the U.S. Senate (2008, 3). *America's Army* is mentioned in this report as one of many U.S. military recruitment methods that, according to the ACLU, target youth under seventeen for future military recruitment. Other interventions and protests periodically positioned *America's Army* as a symbol of military recruitment for unpopular and unjust wars. Joseph DeLappe's *Dead in Iraq* art project and memorial recorded in-game videos of DeLappe typing the names of deceased veterans in the *America's Army* chat log—and the acrimonious reactions many players had to him doing so.[12] His "America's Diplomat" webpage, which modeled the design of the *America's Army* webpage to advertise a fictional game for the U.S. Foreign Service, were among some of the better organized and publicized online interventions.[13]

Despite these instances, which challenged the official messages of *America's Army* in creative and compelling ways, for the most part the game itself avoided controversy and was relegated in mainstream news media to coverage focusing on the novelty of the U.S. Army as a game developer. (As chapter 5 details, the Virtual Army Experience and the Army Experience Center were met with more organized opposition, perhaps due to the fact that they were both in physical, publicly accessible locations.) This general avoidance of controversy was due, in part, to the multiple strategies of persuasion described in this chapter, which were directed at a variety of audiences and institutions. OEMA's efforts were constantly geared toward the end goal of harnessing new "talent" to ensure the future viability of the army. To this end Wardynski focused his efforts on convincing government and military entities about the feasibility of the project. Marketing and public relations experts directed their energies toward convincing the public of the ethical foundation of the game in regards to its depictions of violence, its age-appropriateness, and its game-like portrayals of war. At the same time, the game itself worked to persuade its users to enlist, or at the very least move toward accepting the army as a positive institution shaping American society. In the next chapter I turn to an investigation of some of the specific techniques *America's Army* uses to achieve this result.

3   The Artifice of the Virtual and the Real

We are now subjected to a new super-structure of war fantasy in
which the targets of warfare and the enemies of public safety are as
malleable and as arbitrary as a dream image.

ALLEN FELDMAN, "Deterritorialized Wars of Public Safety"

This enemy is no longer concrete and localizable but has now become
something fleeting and ungraspable, like a snake in the imperial
paradise. The enemy is unknown and unseen and yet ever present,
something like a hostile aura. The face of the enemy appears in the
haze of the future and serves to prop up legitimation where
legitimation has declined. This enemy is in fact not merely elusive but
completely abstract.

MICHAEL HARDT and ANTONIO NEGRI, *Multitude*

While the scenarios of many military war games are fictional, the underlying purpose of *America's Army* is very real. As government adaptations
of *America's Army* software are being used to train soldiers for specific
job-related combat skills, the public video game's goal is, in the words
of one army officer, "filling seats for basic training" by tapping into an
already militarized gaming population. Though the Army Game Project
consistently disavowed any recruitment goals in public relations material surrounding the franchise's products, representatives regularly
acknowledged an explicit recruitment goal privately. The data collected
by OEMA and the rationale articulated by Wardynski in the preceding
chapter also reflect this emphasis. Regardless of whether the game is
effective at achieving this recruitment goal, as a device of a military
institutional power that aims to distribute and normalize the logic of

the military among civil society, *America's Army* seeks to influence how nonenlisted individuals think about the army. These nonenlisted virtual soldiers—the game's civilian designers, its players, the friends and family of these individuals, and even anthropologists who study the game—all have an increased potential to be persuaded through the game to accept the prioritization of U.S. military needs and American militarized narratives as a commonsensical, unquestioned fact. For these reasons, the Army Game Project presents a window into how the army views itself and how it is working to spread its cultural imaginary outward through public relations campaigns, technological spectacle, appeals to masculinity and patriotism, and many other rhetorical deployments.

One type of these deployments—the figure of the mythic, "unreal" enemy—works to enable game users to participate in a kind of ritualistic, virtual subjugation of the constantly morphing and elusive enemies of the United States. These enemies stand in stark contrast to the so-called *America's Army* Real Heroes, nine actual soldiers held up as "aspirational" soldier-citizens by the Army Game Project, who were also made into plastic action figures and featured online. Though modeled on the lives and narratives of actual soldiers, the Real Heroes are public personalities and just as much artificial constructs as the unreal enemy. The noncurated story of one Real Hero, Tommy Rieman, is a contrasting and complex narrative that belies the carefully curated persona of the Real Hero. Taken together the unreal enemy and the Real Hero work in tandem, and are both artifices that perpetuate war.

The Unreal Enemy

As kids my two cousins and I would often play the double game pack of *Super Mario Brothers* and *Duck Hunt*, which came included with the original Nintendo Entertainment System. Even though I, and most other people I knew, enjoyed playing *Mario* more, it was still fun to shoot computerized ducks with the electronic gun that came with the game. There was something about the way the ducks got this goofy, shocked expression in their eyes when shot that we found fun and satisfying. None of us paid much attention to the violence in our game playing, especially since I personally witnessed more actual violence in my cousins' fighting over the right to use the Nintendo gun than I did in shooting goofy ducks or squashing monsters beneath Mario's lethal jump. When not playing video games, we sometimes gained similar pleasures of imaginative destruction when staging immense battles of green, grey, and tan army men, complete with Lincoln Log forts. The enemies in these battles, however, were not abstract, slightly anthropomorphic creatures, but usually ones upon which we all agreed: Nazi Germans and Soviets.

A large portion of video games have generally unobjectionable enemies because they do not exist in the world outside of the imagination: diabolical wizards, goofy cartoon ducks, fire-breathing dragons, invading aliens, oversized human-eating plants, and the list can go on. Although many contemporary games still premise their plots on fighting these more abstract enemies, national enemies that are peculiar to particular historical and cultural circumstances are also evident in many games. These enemies have a history, since they are often preexistent in long-standing cultural narratives that originate outside the game world itself. When my cousins and I played with plastic army men and Lincoln Logs, for example, we were inspired by our watching of American nationalist films, such as *The Dirty Dozen*, *The Green Berets*, and *Patton*. Like these films, which were produced during the Vietnam era, war-themed video games are often valorizations of past or current conflicts that parallel contemporary military endeavors. Just as often, military-themed FPS games are set in the near future, and imagine specific national or ideological enemies against which the American military must fight. A great number of military-themed game franchises follow one of these models. Prominent examples would include those games in the *Battlefield*, *Medal of Honor*, *Call of Duty*, and *Conflict* franchises, as well as *Contra* and *Rush N' Attack* (two examples from the 1980s), and the 2011 game *Homefront*, which envisioned an invasion of the United States by North Korea—thus paralleling the general backstory of the remade film *Red Dawn* (2012), modeled on the original 1984 film of the same name. (Whereas the original *Red Dawn* film posed a pan-Communist enemy consisting mainly of Soviets and Cubans, the remake posits a North Korean enemy backed by Russia.) With increasingly better graphics, modeling, texturing, and motion capture capabilities, these specific enemies become rendered in increasingly minute detail.

Concurrent with this trend toward marking an enemy with a locale, history, and culture, however, has been the continuous presence of other forms of enemy abstraction in military-themed games such as *America's Army*, which presents an anonymous enemy not confined to specific regions or nationalities. The history of war gaming is, generally speaking, a history of generic, abstract enemies, "red vs. blue" configurations in which opposing forces are capable, matched, and malleable according to particular situations. As such, the kinds of enemies within *America's Army* are not entirely new. *America's Army*, likewise, follows well-established conventions for first-person shooter (FPS) gameplay. One reason for this is the game's use of the Unreal game engine, one of the most popular video game engines for first-person shooters. Giving designers a tool to shape the physics within an environment, visually render data, define the behavior of artificial intelligence, and store system files (among many other things), game engines are the backbone around which everything else in a game is layered. *America's Army* was the first game to use the Unreal Engine 2, and its designers attributed part of its early success in 2002 to its presentation of the engine's then cutting-edge graphics, which were made available to gamers for free. *America's Army 3* (AA3), released in June 2009, uses the Unreal Engine 3.

In alluding to the Unreal Engine, I use the term *unreal* to describe the type of enemy appearing in the game and in the examples articulated below. This enemy resides within the uneasy liminal space established by the double entendre in the phrase "the unreal enemy of America's Army." (This phrase can be read a variety of ways, all of which are correct. "Unreal" can refer to the engine, or the adjective, or simultaneously both; "America's Army" can refer to the game, or the military institution, or both.) By using the word *unreal*, I do not mean to connote the negation, opposite, or nonexistence of the "real." The unreal enemy is not so much the mirror or opposite of a "real" enemy as the means through which the actual enemy is engendered and understood.[1] The fictional enemies in military games not only reflect cultural preoccupations and anxieties about future conflict, but also are one way in which actual enemies become manifest. In other words, preparation for fighting potential enemies is one way of summoning them into existence.

This kind of enemy cannot exist without the presence of its opposite (Gallison 1994), which in this case is the American soldier. *America's*

Army provides a salient illustration of this by disallowing gamers to play as the enemy of the U.S. Army. Although the general format of the game consists of two teams of human players that fight against one another—one assaulting while the other defends, typically—the point of view of every human player is that of an American soldier. This unique design in the game, called the "swapping paradigm" by its developers, means that two players on different teams appear to themselves as U.S. soldiers but to one another as enemies. The stipulation that U.S. soldiers are not legitimate targets in the world of *America's Army* is reinforced by the rules of engagement (ROE), which punish players for friendly (and often very unfriendly) fire in the game by removing "honor" points, a factor that can affect a player's level of prestige, access to servers, and selection of more desirable weapons and leadership positions in the game.

Every human player sees his or her opponents as opposing enemy forces, who in the earlier versions of the game wore ski masks or other veiling apparatus for erasing phenotypic markers that might point toward particular ethnicities or groups. In *America's Army 3*, this kind of enemy masking was done away with and both enemy and American soldiers featured the same randomized assortment of faces but drastically different silhouettes and gear. The erasure of a differentiated enemy race aided in the construction of an anonymous enemy potentially anywhere and applicable to any situation. One army recruiter and avid *America's Army* player with whom I spoke made this connection explicitly: "The game teaches you not to shoot at the friendlies. It emphasizes fighting terrorists, not communists or certain nationalities. You don't see their features, so you can't be biased or prejudiced towards any race or group of people. Nothing about the game creates a desire to kill or racist attitudes. It is designed for teamwork and positive attitudes, not negative ones like killing and racism."

Designers of the game certainly made this removal of an identifiable enemy race a deliberate part of the game's design, but it also served other practical purposes regarding the game's playability. An artist, Zeke, indicated that this practice was definitely on purpose.

For one, it's for the reasons that we're talking about [regarding race and nationality]. Two, it's kind of a double plus in our favor because it also gives the enemy a distinguished look from friend. So when you are playing a game like this where it's not always clear—black and white—who you should be shooting at from far away, if there's not distinct things on the character, it's going to be hard. I can only imagine that it's probably like that [in actual combat], if you're not always in contact with where your teammates are in a real battle. [. . .] But that's one of those things where gameplay-wise, we have to make it fun since if it's too hard people are not going to want to play. So things like using ski masks or some crazy weird camo just to make them stand out helps a lot in just distinguishing the enemy, plus there are no implications there. At least that's the goal. I think that all war games get flack from time to time. This one just probably gets more because of the army.

Even though the faces of enemies are visible in the new *America's Army* 3, players are automatically assigned a variety of random faces by the game, and do not typically see their own faces. The variety of geographical markers presented in the game over the years furthermore presupposes an enemy not from any specific region. The environments of the game, such as a snowy wilderness, swamps and farms reminiscent of the Deep South, abandoned eastern European cities, and central Asian terrains that have, in some cases, been modeled directly from landscapes in Afghanistan (Halter 2006, xiv), attest to the universal applicability of the type of enemy that can be of any ethnicity and located in any setting. This enemy is in stark contrast to similar games of the military first-person shooter genre, mentioned above. Rather than externalizing the enemy as, for example, a Russian or an Iraqi "other," the terrains and enemies of *America's Army* imply that the enemy could very well be located internally, within the United States (see figs. 4 and 5).

Zeke further discussed how linguistic and cultural considerations also play a significant factor in the game's presentation, verifying that

making an enemy—that's really hard to do without making a lot of people really upset and pissed off considering it's the army game. [. . .] There's never been a directive; nobody's ever come to me in my office and said things like, "No, you can't put Arabic lettering on this door." I have been told not to use English letters and I've heard references to not using things that make those kinds of implications, but that's also a personal thing—I just don't do that. But it's definitely been said a lot of times in our reviews. And on the flip side of that too, like on U.S. soil stuff, one of the objects I made had lettering in it. It had a made-up brand on it, but I remember in our art review the producers said, "You know, we don't want to use U.S. lettering." We actually have our own made up language. So, for example, a bus that I was working on had "City Transit" written on the side. After talking with the producers about not having U.S. or English lettering or any kind of recognizable language, I have to go to [Samuel], who made a whole pseudo-algorithm for changing things like the letter "L" to this, "Th" combinations to that. It's really neat to actually see the difference, making up a phrase or word and then giving it to him to change it to some crazy other language that is made up.

The release of *America's Army 3* featured such imaginary languages and geographies even more prominently through the creation of a fictional nation, Czervenia.[2] In this vaguely eastern European country, the unreal enemy of *America's Army* became more fully articulated even as it borrowed from a myriad of preexisting geographical landscapes, histories, languages, weapons, and architectures worldwide. Samuel, a game designer, explained how he cobbled together Czervenian, the new fictional nation's language, through online translation technologies:

[The army] wanted to get away from Iraq and all of that. They wanted to create a political situation that didn't exist. [. . .] So basically we took Croatian and Slovenian and eastern European languages that have a Russian influence and combined it with the grammatical structure of Spanish. [. . .] I pull up babelfish.com and dictionary.com and a few other translation websites, and I put a word in there and try to create interesting sounding words out of Spanish and Slovenian usually, or sometimes Czech. Basically I create something that sounds cool and flows well, and if I create a sentence I say the sentence a few times in a ridiculous eastern European accent. If it sounds kinda cool, okay, we use that.

In this way, developers hoped to design a Czervenian scenario that reflected a reality in which the enemy of the U.S. Army was not completely unfamiliar, and drew predominantly on generic Slavic and Baltic influences in creating the game's cultural and geographical background. Although Samuel and most other *America's Army* game developers generally understood that in 2009 the rising assertive power of Putin's Russia was a growing threat in the eyes of many in the U.S. government, they could not have predicted the political events that seemingly summoned a Russian enemy of *America's Army* into existence.

Cultural Slippage between Home and Enemy

With the release of *America's Army 3* in 2009, a new evolution in the figure of the unreal enemy of *America's Army* emerged. Players who downloaded the game were brought into a scenario in which a fictional but vaguely eastern European island resort nation, the Democratic Republic of the Ostregals, was invaded without provocation by its northern nationalist neighbor, Czervenia. In the scenario the army deployed troops to resolve the situation at the request of both the Ostregal government and the United Nations.

The details of this back story were collaboratively crafted and imagined by the game developers in the California office, my primary fieldwork site. They considered Czervenian soldier and civilian points of view: landscapes, architecture, languages, and even Czervenian weapons were all carefully invented to coincide with Czervenian customs and norms. Artists started talking about a "cultural palette" of colors common in Czervenia and the Ostregals. Using Google image searches, they found structures and cities in Spain, the Czech Republic, Slovenia, and other countries that fit their image of Czervenian geography. A Czervenian language (see above) was created based on various existing European languages, and war-torn settings in Iraq, Afghanistan, and elsewhere became references for battlefield environments in the game. (Although an artist told me that he "[did]n't want to get into Googling 'war zones' because you get a lot of messed-up imagery. But there's definitely a look to war zones.") Continuing the tradition of earlier versions of the unreal enemy of *America's Army*, these extrapolations from the actual world were deliberately appropriated in ways that reflect their referents only obliquely. The developers deliberately avoided direct references to Iraq and Afghanistan, and instead sought to create a political situation that could never exist by crafting this new, but vaguely familiar eastern European, theater of conflict.

As previously mentioned, earlier versions of *America's Army* contained anonymous enemies who were commonly veiled in ski masks, had no obvious political agenda, were from no specific location in the world, and were of no apparent religion. The Czervenian enemy was more specific in its Slavic and Russian cultural allusions and borrowed abundantly from Nazi Germany in political ideology. For public and international relations purposes, however, "the Czervenians couldn't be racial supremacists because we're using the same [variety of character] heads on U.S. soldiers," a game designer told me. "We couldn't mention religious conflict either. That was a very specific thing [that the army directed us not to do]."

The design of the Czervenian enemy points toward a desire to idealize past American conflicts without acknowledging the grim realities of American counterinsurgency campaigns in the early twenty-first century. The army required that the Czervenian conflict, unlike actual counterinsurgency conflicts in Iraq and Afghanistan, have as an enemy a conventional, hierarchically organized, and uniformed modern military fully capable of combating the U.S. military toe-to-toe. In other words the Czervenian enemy bears little resemblance to Iraqi insurgents or the Taliban in Afghanistan and Pakistan, who were the primary opponents of the U.S. military at the time of the game's release. Instead, like other after-the-fact romanticizations of past conflicts between the U.S. Army and conventional militaries, the Czervenian conflict plays into a well-established media genre that represents a heroic conflict against a definable enemy with a set ideology, location, and political agenda. It represents the army fighting a just and virtuous war. "I wanted the scenario to be that the army was going to war," Czervenia's primary architect Samuel told me, "and, for once, they were going to war for the right reasons: to protect people and do justice and stop slaughter. [. . .] It's an idealized version of what the army wants itself to be and what politicians want the army to be used for."

Although the current U.S. military counterinsurgency strategy is not focused on conflicts between nation-states and standing armies (U.S. Army 2007), an American romantic desire for a just war against a definable enemy that is being fought "for the right reasons" is arguably strong. As a powerful and clearly aggressive enemy, Czervenia draws upon this nostalgic tendency, but it also evokes the potentialities of future conflicts by playing into premediated American anxieties over the rising international economic, diplomatic, and military power of long-standing rival and former enemy nations—especially Russia.

This general anxiety is perhaps the reason that, despite careful efforts to distance Czervenia from any real-world nation, the fiction of Czervenia appeared to materialize instantaneously when Russia invaded its southern neighbor, the post-Soviet nation of Georgia, in August 2008. When Wardynski came to visit the California studio one month later, he and the developers expressed concern since it was (in their eyes) uncanny how much Czervenia resembled Russia and how the Democratic Republic of the Ostregals resembled Georgia. "It's almost the exact same scenario," one person told me. There was genuine concern that the unreal, abstract Czervenian enemy could morph into something tangible with real political implications once the game was released. By the time this international event took place, Czervenia had become completely articulated in both the game and the *America's Army Graphic Novel* (see fig. 6), although both were months away from being released. A developer reassured some army visitors to the studio that "the Ostregals are *not* Georgia, although we are probably going to get folks who say things like, 'Those mountains look like the Caucasus!'" In an effort to further distance the game from the Russian-Georgian conflict, specific imagery that could be interpreted as pointing toward this scenario, for example missiles perceived as "too Soviet-looking" were removed or altered at the request of Wardynski.

Curiously the game ARMA 2 (2009), a commercially produced and military-themed competitor game to *America's Army 3* that was released the same year, presented a different type of enemy that embraced these very same events. Marketing itself as containing a storyline "which blurs the boundaries between fact and fiction," ARMA 2 presents a scenario in which a breakaway Communist faction seizes control of a region within the fictional "post-Soviet" Caucasus nation of Chenarus (literally, "Black

Russia"). Without hiding any allusions to the Georgian region of South Ossetia, in the game world of *ARMA 2* the conflict takes place in a region dubbed South Zagoria. The "pro-Western" government of Chenarus predictably calls on NATO for aid, which provides enough shallow justification for U.S. military intervention.

By the time both games were released in June 2009, the Georgian conflict had become largely forgotten in the amnesiac twenty-four-hour news cycle. Czervenia, constructed with the intention of dissociating the U.S. Army from a specific enemy, was nevertheless shown to have an unwelcome potential to be conjured into a particular real-world foe despite the best efforts of its developers. Comparable situations occurred earlier in the history of *America's Army* during the invasion of Iraq in 2003, when some players of the game came to feel the simultaneous resemblance and disparity between the unreal and the actual enemies of the U.S. Army (Li 2003). Other *America's Army* media campaigns have deliberately played on this juxtaposition between representational fidelity and narrative disjunction. This uncanny sense of interconnectedness led Walker, a game developer who had been using a made-up ethnic slur while playing against Czervenians,[3] to pause and jokingly ask me during one of our countless play-test sessions in the development office, "Is it racist to use a slur against a fictional enemy that you invented?"

Henry Jenkins writes that "we use games to work through the intense anxieties surrounding modern warfare, to bring it at least momentarily under our symbolic control" (2003). The construction of an anonymous but proximal enemy, complete with its own ambiguous language, is one institutionalized effort at achieving a symbolic supremacy over potential enemies, and the practice of enemy abstraction is entirely in keeping with a long tradition of war simulation and tactical training exercises of the U.S. military (Der Derian 2001; Dunnigan 1992; Lenoir and Lowood 2005). Such types of enemies enable training to take place against a generic enemy for the purposes of teaching military tactics and doctrine, and ideally produce a more versatile force of soldiers ready to fight any particular foe. They also typically attempt to avoid the general stereotyping of a particular enemy of the United States and the political conundrums that would result from such depictions. In the aftermath of the 2013–14 Euromaidan uprising in Kiev, Ukraine; the Russian annexation of Crimea; and alleged Russian interference in the 2016 U.S. presidential election, American anxieties over Russia have swelled beyond the levels reached during the 2008 Russian war in Georgia and the Caucasus. In popular media the old foe Russia, long depicted in Cold War–era films that remain a part of American war lore, returns now with a new urgency. The unreal enemy harnesses these anxieties, and the fiction of Czervenia provides a politically expedient and militarized arena for their subduing.

My own limited experiences with these kinds of unreal enemies outside of video games have been humorous but revealing. When taking an introductory Reserve Officers' Training Corps (ROTC) course at the University of Washington as part of my preliminary fieldwork for this project, I participated with my fellow classmates in several similar exercises of imagination that enable cadets to hone their abilities to effectively communicate the roles of combat units to all divisional levels in a standardized OPORD (operational order) format. My classmates, when given an open-ended option to create a scenario to practice the OPORD format of communication, envisioned an enemy of pecan-stealing squirrels with high morale, extra sharp teeth and claws, tails that stung like scorpions, and rabies. Virtual combat with the squirrels extended from campus into the fraternity houses, and the cadets, armed with Axe body spray,[4] peanuts, and a new secret drug that would allow them to jump into the trees, eventually subdued the enemy animals.

In anthropologist Catherine Lutz's book *Homefront*, larger and more serious soldier training exercises are examined as connecting points between the symbiotic histories of Fayetteville, North Carolina, and adjacent Fort Bragg and Pope Air Force Base (2001, 87–130). Lutz examines the impact of large-scale simulation exercises that often take place off-base and with the collaboration of civilians. These live simulations, which envision in great socioeconomic and cultural detail a territory called "Pineland," are further described by Anna Simons (1997), also a military anthropologist.[5] Both Lutz and Simons describe how local civilian populations aid in these war simulations by role-playing as guerrillas or citizens of Pineland. In the same way that the languages, landscapes, and enemies of *America's Army* are modeled from generalized locations, Pineland is intentionally a vague but recognizable place, mirroring the surroundings of Fayetteville and constructing what Lutz calls a "mythic" model of the enemy and the world that plays out "culturally tutored imagination, fears, and wishes . . . as if to tame them" (2001, 87).

Pineland, Czervenia, and rabid squirrels terrorizing frat boys each present enemies of mythic proportions and of varying degrees of seriousness. Each type of simulation is imbued with a military imperative to act and subdue threats, and each is a ritual for establishing control over an unknown "other" as much as it is a scenario for military instruction and training. The unreal enemy is an enemy with minimal cultural, linguistic, or ethnic indicators and therefore, though anonymous, might be anyone. Everywhere and nowhere at once, the unreal enemy is a tabula rasa on which any enemy can be extrapolated. For Lutz this type of "unreality in which war games swim . . . has posed special challenges to the separation between foreign and domestic use of force and has potentially allowed cultural slippage between home and enemy" (2001, 103–4).

I found this slippage to be very visible at particular moments during the course of my fieldwork—when I played *America's Army* as a U.S. soldier fighting enemies in landscapes that appear uncannily similar to the surroundings of my birthplace of East Tennessee; when I sat among a class of ROTC cadets who imagine the campus of the University of Washington and its surroundings as a backdrop for wars against bloodthirsty squirrels; when I spoke with the game designers of *America's Army* about the careful attention they must give to erase specific identifiable cultural backgrounds from their enemies; and when I studied the techniques for mapping the nation of Pineland onto the preexisting geographies of Fayetteville.

This slippage is the stuff of the unreal. Though Lutz asserts that these kinds of "ludic moments" of "war game spectatorship" have "redefine[d] the role of the citizen from one who questions and acts to one who observes and is entertained by the state and by power itself" (2001, 107, 109), her stance assumes a unidirectional model of mass media, broadcast from one central power to many individuals in the manner of traditional propaganda and passive viewing. This stance does not take into account the performative and interactive nature of digital media as a means for institutional power to engage the public. The unreal enemy is an enemy that is by definition enacted and performed and not one that is merely experienced by passive spectators. The medium of the video game demands this kind of cybernetic performativity, and the army encourages it in ways that reach beyond the game.

In bringing its message to the public, the Army Game Project accumulated a history of live staged performances, the first of which occurred in 2002 at the Electronic Entertainment Expo (E3), where *America's Army* burst into the gaming world with much critical acclaim, as well as a front-page profile of the game in the *LA Times* (Pham 2002). At the 2003 E3 soldiers rappelled from Black Hawk helicopters down the side of the Los Angeles Convention Center to storm the building (Halter 2006, vii–xi). Later E3 army appearances included a daily morning staging of Golden Knights specialist parachutists jumping 2,500 feet from a Chinook helicopter into a parking lot near the expo, followed by evening shows in which Special Forces soldiers used a converted auto dealership to stage a live-action performance of a mission taken from the game, using "real equipment, weapons, and uniforms" (Larkin 2005). Other early public exposures to *America's Army* at expositions such as the Yerba Buena Center for the Arts further emphasized the fidelity between in-game elements and actual army weapons and practices through exhibits that combined virtual and physical environments in intriguing ways (Chapman 2004; Davis and Bossant 2004).[6] Similar types of domestic invasions were implemented through the Virtual Army Experience, which "deployed" (using Army Game Project wording in press releases) to large public events across the United States. The Army Experience Center in Philadelphia was a related two-year pilot project in recruitment via new media, community outreach, and the "soft sell."

These performed domestic invasions bypass much of the virtual-real binary often encountered in popular and academic discussions about digital games and call into question the utility of such binaries (see chapter 1). The army itself blurred the line between the real and the virtual, supplying an in-game "Virtual Recruiting Station" that players could visit to learn more about so-called *America's Army* Real Heroes, individuals chosen to represent an ideal of personal achievement and service who are upheld as model soldiers, typically noncommissioned officers at levels of rank that were realistically attainable by dedicated recruits (see fig. 7). Such visits potentially provided visitors with a wealth of information on specific Military Occupational Specialties (MOS), uniform decorations, and individual biographies of enlisted soldiers. In contrast to the unreal enemy in *America's Army*, players were encouraged to connect with these Real Heroes and were rewarded with bonus "honor points" for visiting the Virtual Recruiting Station. Three-inch plastic figurines depicting each Real Hero were distributed as promotional merchandise, and several of the actual Real Heroes toured the country with the Virtual Army Experience, making public appearances at air shows, NASCAR races, state fairs, and other large public events.

The Real Heroes, as individuals, stand in opposition to the abstraction of the unreal enemy. Although *America's Army* is not a role-playing game (RPG) as typically defined in most taxonomies of video games, the game encouraged players to emulate the Real Heroes as "aspirational figures" (Wardynski 2007), and its developers consciously sought to incorporate more role-playing elements into *America's Army 3*. Plans for another *America's Army* game, subtitled *Soldiers*, which was to be more exclusively focused on role-playing a career path through the army, were discontinued in the early stages of the project, but the desire on the part of the developers to include role-playing elements within the game has influenced later versions and spin-offs such as the Virtual Army Experience and the Army Experience Center, both of which are venues that emphasize the specific job functions of military occupational specialties (MOS). The *America's Army* chief operations officer at OEMA, Maj. Mike Marty, also described the reasons for implementing the Real Heroes program in these terms, telling me during a visit to West Point that "[the army has] less elbow-to-elbow contact with the average citizens of America. Because of that, there are fewer opportunities for the army to sell itself. You can't do that in a thirty-second commercial. You've got to provide them with a virtual world where they can rub elbows with soldiers and with the army instead of having other people tell them what the army is."

In the context of the game, players can become "real heroes" themselves, and perhaps it is in this ambiguity between soldier and player, in the liminality of the virtual soldier, that the efficacy of the game as a public-relations tool is the most profound and obvious. Individual players, for example, were periodically upheld by the Army Game Project as model citizens, as was the case when an *America's Army* player provided medical aid at a car accident. He credited the basic medical training that all players of versions of the game (prior to *America's Army 3*) had to sit through to play the game—a fifteen-minute lecture in a virtual classroom—as being crucial to his ability to care for the victim of the car crash until emergency help arrived. In a press release Wardynski called this player a "true hero," adding, "we are pleased to have played a role in providing the lifesaving training that he employed so successfully at the scene" (Army Game Project 2008). Another enlisted soldier added to this rhetorical blending between in-game action and its referents in an interview, explaining to me that "everything is realistic in the game because it was designed entirely by the army. Even the medic is real life."[7]

Enlisted soldiers, though, are the ones who are ultimately presented as being the "real heroes" and the "true soldiers." (A console version of the game was titled *America's Army: True Soldiers*.) The *America's Army* website periodically published articles featuring biographical information about the Real Heroes—including personal photos of their families, detailed information of badges and awards that each Real Hero has received, and video interview footage. Stories of the singular combat experience for which they were awarded medals are the predominant characteristic of these biographies.[8] In one such description, an interview article published originally at the *America's Army* website revisits Real Hero Gerald Wolford's experience of being fired on by an Iraqi adversary:

> "My gunner and I both saw an RPG [rocket-propelled grenade] fired at our position, and I had time to turn and yell 'RPG!' so the two other men had time to get down." The RPG hit the bridge right above the HMMWV [Humvee], wounding two of Wolford's men. [. . .] Since his HMMWV had only suffered minor damage from the RPG blast, Wolford used it to shield his wounded Soldiers as he moved them to the casualty collection point and into the care of the medics. Refusing medical care for his injuries, Wolford moved forward once again, so as to provide his men with cover. "At this time," he says, "the vehicle got hit by the second RPG. [. . .] [W]e didn't even see the guy that fired

it." [. . .] Just as the attacker readied another RPG, he was spotted by the Americans. Wolford observes the attacker, "He must have thought he was bulletproof. He knelt down in the middle of the road, and dropped another round in it. We engaged him, and we didn't have to worry about that RPG anymore."[9]

Here the Real Hero's language does the work of abstracting an Iraqi enemy into an inanimate object that acts as an unreal enemy: instead of worrying about the Iraqi soldier, the RPG is the enemy to be worried about. These accounts by the Real Heroes, which attempt to define and interpret the gaming experience, enable a valorization of the figure of the soldier that is not merely unidirectional, but enacted and cybernetic—as is any game. The correspondence between the acronyms for "rocket-propelled grenade" and "role-playing game" is, of course, a coincidence, but this correspondence aptly captures the slippage at work between technomilitary and gamer jargon, and that between a domesticated genre of games and a tool of the enemy. Both are used and abbreviated as a technology of war. From the point of view of military institutional power, both kinds of RPGs are, in a sense, weapons.

Just as the Real Heroes are useful to the army in enabling players to emulate and envision themselves in their position, the unreal enemy is a useful way for the military to envision its targets. In contrast to other military-themed shooters, with enemies from a specific location in space and time, *America's Army* provides little in the way of conceptualizing the enemy within temporal or spatial fields. The unreal enemy of *America's Army* is a return to enemy abstraction; it is an abstraction, however, that is not based on computing limitations or aesthetic choices in design, but one that is more pervasive and encompassing of both in-game and out-of-game contexts. Nameless, elusive, and always just around the corner, the unreal enemy is not confined to any single game or moment. The unreal enemy influences and precedes the production of actual enemies of the U.S. Army and operates within the framework of military institutional power, producing through virtual soldiering a "hybrid subjectivity" that is constituted "outside the institutions but even more intensely ruled by their disciplinary logics" (Hardt and Negri 2000, 330–32).

Due to its abstraction, the constructed nature of the unreal enemy is immediately obvious. The Real Heroes, however, also participate in a narrative process that constructs the entirety of their lives around a particular moment—the moment of combat when their deeds elevated them to become a Real Hero. These deeds, the messaging implies, are deeds that anyone can perform if he or she has the military discipline, training, and courage, but it is this performance that distinguishes the Real Hero from the ordinary individual. The Real Heroes were ultimately a way of challenging and seeking to change the "cog in a wheel," industrial Fordist image of the army. Like the army's short-lived, contradictory, and Rambo-evoking failure of a slogan, "Army of One," the Real Heroes sought to portray to civilians (and potential recruits) that the army was composed of a multitude of "talented" soldiers, not a mass of "grunts." "Empower yourself, defend freedom" is a phrase that appears on many Army Game Project products, and the Real Heroes embodied this discourse of individual empowerment within the total institution of the army.

Websites, blogs, personal photos, bios, videos, press interviews, and appearances at the Virtual Army Experience all play a role in the multimedia effort to personalize the army through the individual figures of Real Heroes. And yet beneath the public persona of the Real Hero, there naturally exists a more indeterminate human figure. As in the case of the unreal enemy, the construction of the identity of a Real Hero is in its own way an artifice that curates and omits other aspects of their lives that may not be the most flattering to the U.S. Army. The intrepid deeds performed and experienced by Real Heroes are indeed life-changing events that differentiate them from most other people, but not necessarily in the ways portrayed in *America's Army* messaging.

When I spoke with Real Hero Tommy Rieman, the Real Heroes program coordinator, this disjunction became readily apparent in his account of his postdeployment adjustment and his ongoing experiences with post-traumatic stress disorder (PTSD) that began almost immediately after his return from Iraq to the United States. In contrast to his public persona, Rieman's own account of his enlistment and return is an ambivalent one that tells of simultaneous disillusionment and patriotic pride, and contains within it elements that are consciously omitted from the highly sanitized and polished public Real Hero narrative.

Rieman's story of deployment, trauma, reenlistment, and redeployment two years after my 2008 conversation with him is featured in the documentary *Halfway Home* (2013). The film focuses on the institutional and sociocultural barriers that prevent injured veterans from overcoming the traumatic experiences of war. It recreates an overarching discursive take on PTSD that problematizes government institutions more than the practices of American war and the ideological positions that justify it. PTSD, the film implies, is a necessary but unfortunate price to pay for ensuring the freedom of Americans, and it can be overcome with better institutional support and civilian volunteer efforts. The film humanizes each of the five individuals it profiles in meaningful ways, but its overall message is that empathy for injured veterans goes hand-in-hand with support for war. Opposition to war, the film implies, is the same as opposing the injured veterans like Rieman who return having experienced life-changing trauma.

PTSD, however, plays no part in the stories of Real Hero media personalities. Notably, no Real Hero has any visual physical index of injury, as this would be counterproductive to the Army Game Project recruitment goals (see fig. 8). Communications scholar Paul Achter discusses Rieman in an analysis of media representations of the bodies of injured American war veterans, writing that "as far as the visual record is concerned, Rieman [has] traveled to the brink of death and returned unscathed, making [him a] useful [representation] of America, of the army, and of the warrior spirit the military likes to cultivate in new recruits" (2010, 53).

Rieman, however, is more than simply that, as I quickly discovered during the Indianapolis Air Show in 2008, when I sat down with him at a desk behind the driver's seat of one of the air-conditioned Virtual Army Experience semitrailers. As I was going through required protocol for explaining informed consent for use of interview material, he began staring me down deadpan, looking for all the world like he was ready to fight me. Flustered, I raised my eyebrow questioningly, and he broke into a smile that made me laugh: "Just kidding!" he said.

Rieman joined the army when he was seventeen, in 1999, one month after his graduation from high school. He was assigned first to the Eighty-Second Airborne Division and later to the Fifty-First Infantry, and was stationed at different times at Fort Bragg (the home of Pineland), in Kosovo, and in Germany. Before he was deployed to Iraq he joined a unit specializing in Long-Range Surveillance (LRS). Several days prior to the ground invasion of Iraq in March 2003, this unit was paradropped within Iraqi territory for reconnaissance and the calling-in of air strikes on Iraqi military positions. He and his squad of five others were, in his words, "sittin' in a LRS hide-site for seven fuckin' days. You can't move, your buddy's holding your MRE (Meal Ready to Eat) bag so you can shit in it because you can't move, 'cause you're stuck in this fuckin' hole. Cold as shit, feet wet, almost getting hypothermia." Despite the harsh conditions, Rieman recalls this particular experience of martial camaraderie as one of the best memories of his military career.

Almost four years later, near the end of the 2007 State of the Union address, President George W. Bush, instigator of the Iraq War, paid tribute to Tommy Rieman, who sat two seats away from First Lady Laura Bush throughout the speech. The president's comments mirrored the sterile combat narratives of other *America's Army* Real Heroes (see above). Bush described the particular events that happened nine months after Rieman's LRS reconnaissance mission—events that have defined his army career and much of his life ever since—in the following way:

> Tommy Rieman was a teenager pumping gas in Independence, Kentucky, when he enlisted in the U.S. Army. In December 2003 he was on a reconnaissance mission in Iraq when his team came under heavy enemy fire. From his Humvee Sergeant Rieman returned fire. He used his body as a shield to protect his gunner. He was shot in the chest and the arm, and received shrapnel wounds to his legs, yet he refused medical attention and stayed in the fight. He helped to repel a second attack, firing grenades at the enemy's position. For his exceptional courage, Sergeant Rieman was awarded the Silver Star.[10]

Having killed an unspecified number of Iraqi insurgents, Rieman affirms, "I think about December 3, 2003, every day of my life. . . . [I]t continues to haunt me" (Freedman 2013). Given continuing unofficial attitudes in the military that stigmatize PTSD, Rieman's candor and honesty in discussing his experiences and publicly bringing attention to the need for critical changes in institutional and social attitudes toward such life-altering war trauma as PTSD is courageous.

The day following the events described by President Bush, Rieman was medevac'd out of Iraq, "strapped down to a cot, and flown all the way back to fuckin' Walter Reed, and Walter Reed down to Fort Bragg, [North Carolina]." Rieman was reunited with his wife and had "a great weekend, I'm so excited, I'm like, 'Hell yeah, this is how we roll.' They give us a fuckin' weekend off, I get recovery leave, they give me plenty of medication and shit for the weekend." After this initial positive homecoming, however, he underwent "some of the worst processes in my life." He was ordered to report to a unit in Fort Bragg but did not have a physical copy of his orders or any contact numbers for obtaining them. He showed up on the following Monday,

> and I swear to God it was like I had three dicks on my forehead, 'cause nobody would fuckin' help me because I didn't have a piece of paper. Basically they said, "Who the fuck are you? Where are you from? If you don't have orders, we can't help you." [. . .] Unfortunately, the army can make the same mistakes. And it's just like any Fortune 500 company, you know, it's a huge powerhouse, an organization. 1.5 million employees, scattered all over the world. I mean, we're really damn good at what we do, but unfortunately people slip through the cracks and things happen. Things aren't set up, and we don't learn from our mistakes. When I was wounded, there wasn't any wounded warrior program set up.

Rieman had severe difficulties in obtaining medical treatment, especially psychological treatment, "which is insane." He tried to stop the army's finance offices from paying him extra tax-free payments for being in Iraq, "and they said, 'We can't help you, you don't have orders.' And I was like, 'You know, I'm trying to stop you guys from paying me too much.' 'Sorry, I can't help you.' That's what I got." Rieman dealt with these issues and an increasingly difficult marriage

> for months. I didn't have a psychologist to talk to. It was the hardest time in my life, becoming sensitive again, because you're totally ster-

ile over there. You lose feelings and emotions to a point. You become numb to certain things. The slightest things when I came back would scare me, and I didn't know how to communicate with my wife. She went through a life-changing event by running the household and taking care of everything and living with the stress of not having me there. And then, I was there. And how do you explain it to one another to let them understand? You have to really, really communicate and you have to do it well. [We] did not communicate well at all. So. We'd say things, and they'd be the same thing, but we would say it in such different ways that . . . [Allen: It just misses?] Yeah. That was the hardest part, just reintegrating myself back into civilian life.

I didn't have a unit to report to, so everyday I'd just sit at my house and be with my family and live with that [experience] every night. You have nightmares, you wake up sweating, you're screaming, you're crying, you're . . . And you find yourself waking up in the bathtub, or outside. I'd be freaking out, locking the doors, paranoid as fuck. We'd be out at Wal-Mart and all of these people and you'd just want to fuckin' explode on somebody. There's a bag in the road, and you swerve, or . . . I remember one night distinctly: we were driving back into our neighborhood and there was a lake. Somebody had let off some serious fireworks, and I was driving. You know, we got hit with IEDs (Improvised Explosive Devices) in Iraq. I was driving and those fireworks went off. I swerved off [the road], and the front tire got stuck in the lake. I got out and ran out of the fuckin' vehicle and dove into the woods, and my wife just sat there and looked at me like I was the craziest motherfucker on the planet. It took me a minute to step back and say, "Holy shit!" So reintegrating just wasn't easy.

After Rieman had been facing these experiences of PTSD for several months without any consistent medical support, his unit returned from Iraq and he was finally able to contact it to obtain his orders and paperwork. He went to check in and introduced himself:

They treat me like shit: "Where the fuck have you been? Why are you so fat?" I gained sixty-five pounds after I got back, [and] I was fucked up. I couldn't go out and exercise, I didn't have any motivation. I thought that the army had forgotten about me, that they didn't give a shit about me, and that was really hard for me to take. And I hated that because I love the army, absolutely love it. [. . .] I'd tell them my story [but] they thought I was lying because I didn't have paperwork to prove it.

These difficulties went on for eight months, until August 2004, when Rieman unexpectedly received a package in the mail, containing the Silver Star and Purple Heart medals. "I didn't think I did anything special, and I was nominated by everybody on my team." Once the medals arrived, the attitudes of his fellow soldiers at Fort Bragg changed:

People were lickin' my nuts after that because they couldn't believe that I was telling the truth the whole time, that it wasn't a lie, and that the paperwork was there. [. . .] The army sticks to their rules, [and] if it's common sense approachable, but a not-so-common issue, people lock up and don't know what to do. They say, "Hell, I'm a soldier, that's the rules." No, hold on. I understand rules are guidelines, but let's take a look at this. We're soldiers, we're people, let's take care of each other.

After these experiences Rieman was seriously considering not renewing his enlistment and looking for employment outside the army. The medals, however, were in his eyes a message from the army that his sacrifice was recognized and appreciated. He recounted to me a conversation that he had, after receiving the medals, with an army general,

a division commander for the Eighty-Second. He said, "Son, there's no fuckin' way you should get out of the army. It would be crazy. You've done so many great things—what can I do for you?" And I said, "Not a fuckin' thing, sir." Just like that. And he goes, "Well, are you bitter?" And I said, "Well, a little bit." I say, "Sir, it's going to take an act of God for me to stay in the army," and he goes, "What if I get you assigned to the Pentagon as security for the secretary of defense?" I said, "Okay—where do I sign?" Just like that. Two days later, he had paperwork, I signed and reenlisted. Two weeks before I get [to the Pentagon], I get this call [. . .], "We're really excited about you coming to the office and stuff." I was like, "Yeah, I'm pretty excited to protect the secretary." And she goes, "Protect the secretary? It's not a hazardous job or anything. Our secretary is fine."

Instead of being assigned to the promised position, Rieman had been placed in a personnel job, dealing primarily in human resources, "which for an infantry grunt [. . .] is pretty rough to adjust to." It was in this work at the Pentagon that he met Wardynski, who asked him to become part of the new Real Heroes program, becoming a spokesperson for both *America's Army* and, by extension, the U.S. Army. In 2007 he withdrew from active duty to join the Virginia National Guard but continued to participate in the Real Heroes program by attending events such as the VAE (see chapter 5), where I met him in Indianapolis. Although he understood the need to seek psychological help, especially after his initial return to the United States, Rieman continued to have trouble with unaddressed issues stemming from his PTSD. He did not consider the available counselors capable of understanding his suffering and facilitating any recovery, since they had not experienced overseas deployment in war zones themselves. His marriage ended in divorce.

Two years after my 2008 interview with him Rieman was once again called up for deployment to Iraq. *Halfway Home* details how he thought that this experience of returning to war might help him come to terms with the persistent traumatic consequences of his last deployment. Rieman's return to the crucible of war during this second tour in Iraq, though, further contributed to unaddressed feelings of isolation, depression, and powerlessness. At one haunting moment in the documentary he recounts how he removed the photos of his children and girlfriend from the walls of his barracks room, loaded his rifle, placed the barrel in his mouth, and sat on his bed, switching the safety from on to off repeatedly. While this moment of contemplating suicide was not his first, it was a turning point for Rieman, who decided at that moment that he would not be overcome by his own sense of helplessness. While still deployed he finally sought out (and was able to receive) long-term counseling and medical help. Rieman has since become a public figure in speaking out about veteran's needs, especially regarding medical treatment and counseling.

In the eyes of many, Rieman's soldiering narrative might provide powerful and tangible evidence to invoke as justification against military enlistment. Having endured parallel conditions of war trauma, other soldiers have evolved in their interpretations of their enlistment experiences to positions of resistance, to the point of refusing deployment orders (Gutmann and Lutz 2010). Rieman, however, changed in a contrasting way, and despite his negative experiences chose to become an archetypal representative of the army. Echoing Bush's State of the Union speech, he framed his military work experiences as a classic heroic war narrative of masculine camaraderie and "selfless service." Rieman told me that he looked positively on what "the army has structurally done for me as a man, and showed me the ways of life—and also *showed* me life. [. . .] If you can just put it past yourself—it's not about you, it's about you serving your fuckin' country and looking to your brother left and right and serving with them."

He then paused to address me directly: "If you have a son and he goes and joins the army, I guarantee that you would feel guilty that you never did. This is why I do it. I serve because of my kids. I want to be able to say that I served, so he doesn't if he doesn't want to. Or, I go fight this battle so he doesn't have to and he's safe. [. . .] [I]t's pride when you wear this uniform.[11] So much shit has happened to me and I still love the army," he told me, "so if all that can happen to me and I can love it, it's fuckin' great. And I want to change people's lives. The army will." The question, however, remains as to the manner in which one's life potentially changes as a result of enlistment. If *America's Army* is indeed providing the "whole damn book" (to use Wardynski's own phrasing) about the U.S. Army and the labor of war, the disturbing aftermath of Rieman's story following his defining Real Hero combat events would be a part of it.

As things were, though, the Real Hero and the actual Tommy Rieman were two very different personas who, when contrasted, reveal what U.S. historian James Loewen describes as a process of "heroification" that turns "flesh-and-blood individuals into pious, perfect creatures without conflicts, pain, credibility, or human interest" (2007, 11). It is precisely the "flesh-and-blood" human qualities of Rieman's powerful personal narrative that were omitted from his Real Hero character, which became sanitized as a plastic G.I. Joe type of action figure, devoid of personality, injuries, and flaws. This work of morphing a real human being into an "aspirational figure" parallels other tendencies in American historical memory to "reduce heroes from dramatic men and women to melodramatic stick figures. Their inner struggles disappear" (Loewen 2007, 29). This, too, is the work of militarization, for the highly scripted, half-truthful war narratives of the Real Heroes obscure and deflect attention away from the trauma inflicted on both soldiers and their families, friends, and extended communities.

The figure of the unreal enemy provides for an omnipresent and formidable danger that the Real Hero unselfishly struggles against and ultimately vanquishes. This artificial framework repositions the threats posed to the legitimacy of the military by the unruliness of the bodies of injured soldiers, and reconstitutes the Real Hero and *America's Army* as an ostensibly safe domain that can be inscribed and coded with institutional messages. The creation of these kinds of institutional "safe domains" was a critical aspect of the recruitment goals of *America's Army* and its franchise products, and a central element of the "soft sell" atmosphere cultivated at venues such as the Virtual Army Experience (vae) and the Army Experience Center (aec)—both of which I explore in the next chapter.

1. In-game marketing image for the "Alley" level of *America's Army 3*.

2. The outside entrance to the Office of
Economic and Manpower Analysis.
Photo by the author, September 2006.

3. *America's Army* Real Heroes Tommy Rieman (*left*) and John Adams (*center*) being interviewed at the Virtual Army Experience by CNN correspondent Susan Roesgen for *The Situation Room with Wolf Blitzer*. Photo by the author, August 2008.

4. A reference photo, used by *America's Army* level designers and artists, of a house in the rural United States.

5. The reference photo's in-game application in the "Ranch" scenario of *America's Army 3*.

6. The front cover to issue 8 of the *America's Army Graphic Novel* series, featuring the Czervenian leader President-General Azdic. Sherman, Brooks, and Brown 2013.

7. One of the Real Heroes of *America's Army*, sfc Gerald Wolford, in digital, plastic, and photographic representation.

8. Tommy Rieman's Real Hero action figure. Photo by the author.

9. An exterior view of the VAE Alpha at the Indianapolis Air Show.
Photo by the author.

10. A mock-up life-size Humvee inside the
VAE. Photo by the author.

11. Drill sergeants provide entertainment for visitors waiting in line outside the VAE by challenging them with push-ups for army gear. Photo by the author.

12. Real Heroes Tommy Rieman and John Adams sign free copies of the *America's Army* video game given to visitors as they exit. Photo by the author.

13. A typical gaming scenario at AEC computers. A variety of games were available to play, including the most current versions of *America's Army*, *World of Warcraft*, and other sports, role-playing, and first-person shooting games. Photo courtesy of the U.S. Department of Defense.

14. (*Left*) "Grab a bite." An advertisement for the Army Experience Center in the Franklin Mills Mall, Philadelphia. Photo by the author.

15. (*Below left*) Ignited poster advertising the release of *America's Army 3* at the 2009 Game Developers Conference. Photo by the author.

16. (*Below right*) *America's Army* arcade game, published by Global VR.

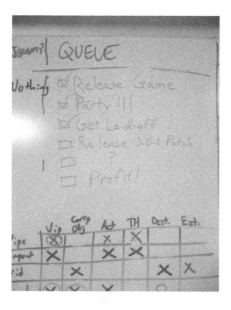

17. (*Above*) Virtual soldiers: civilian *America's Army* video game developers at mini Basic Combat Training. Photo by the Army Game Project.

18. (*Left*) Image from the development office the day of the layoffs. Photo by the author.

4 The Full-Spectrum Soft Sell of the Army Experience

There's this [TV] commercial that shows a Marine climbing some crazy cliff with no gear, and then he fights a dragon and converts into a Marine officer with a sword and everything.[1] Now, you tell me which is a more accurate depiction of the military—a Marine fighting a dragon or a video game that really makes as much effort as possible to be accurate in its depictions of combat and military life? I don't think that [commercial is] a very accurate depiction of what it's like to be a Marine. I think playing a video game is also a far-fetched vision of what it's like to be in the military; however, that being said, our game does genuinely try to portray certain parts of the military. So I do appreciate that, and I think that on some level it is more accurate. But I also feel like there are levels of lying, you know what I mean?

MARCUS, *America's Army* game developer, personal interview

Among brown, arid mountains a scene repeats itself ceaselessly: video news reports tell us that "a well-armed genocidal faction in the city of Nradreg has surrounded a group of humanitarian aid workers and refugees who face starvation and imminent attack. This enemy faction has rejected all diplomatic efforts to negotiate safe passage of relief supplies. As part of international relief efforts, a combined U.S. Army air, sea, and ground task force has been ordered to use appropriate force to reach the remote compound." Helicopters swoop, missiles fly, and, after seven minutes of intense fighting, a convoy of troops arrives with supplies. The unnamed enemy lies defeated. But, as if caught in a time warp, minutes later this Sisyphean scenario begins anew.

This generic conflict against an unreal enemy is the backstory to the cinematic action inside the Virtual Army Experience (VAE). The VAE was one development in the army's push to market itself in a new, positive light, and it was unabashedly an aid to army recruitment. This "mobile mission simulator" was open to the public at locations across the United States from 2007 to 2010 and presented a kinetically engaging battle scenario to individuals who visit large public events (see fig. 9). These events were often air shows featuring well-known military show teams such as the army's Golden Knights, the navy's Blue Angels, and the air force's Thunderbirds. The VAE also visited NASCAR races, as well as fairs, theme parks, and other festivals, but OEMA later determined that NASCAR venues were not optimal sites for the VAE in terms of reaching a recruitable population due to the older and relatively more affluent demographic of fans who purchase race tickets.

The peak activity of the VAE occurred during the 2007 and 2008 tours, when at least three simulators toured nationwide for up to eight months each year. Following the economic crisis that began in 2008, when recruitment became easier due to financial hardships and military budgets shrank slightly, the VAE scaled down to a single-month tour in 2010 and eventually closed permanently. This happened despite the endorsement by Congress in 2010, which commended the army

> for investing in new technological approaches to increase awareness and knowledge of the military among recruitment-age youth. The Army Experience Center in Philadelphia, Pennsylvania, and its transportable counterpart, the Virtual Army Experience, are examples of technological projects that hold great potential to reshape recruiting techniques and conduct recruiting operations on a more cost effective basis. The committee believes this type of investment is essential if the Army intends to keep pace with societal changes regarding the subjects that capture the attention of young people and methods young people use to gather information and socially interact. . . . The committee understands that during periods when recruiting is relatively easy, investment in experimental programs draws increased scrutiny. The committee urges the Army to continue to use these tools and to invest in other related projects to maximize their immediate value, and learn more about how the Army may further adapt technology

to harness the power of the information age to support the recruiting mission. (U.S. Congress 2010, 318)

The VAE and AEC were two programs implemented by the Los Angeles–based marketing agency Ignited, and both were pioneering venues in the army's experimentation with "soft sell" marketing for military recruitment.[2] (On an informational blurb at Ignited's website in 2009, Ignited claimed, "We are in the business of making our clients part of the cultural dialogue and the collective consciousness.") Such tactics implicitly challenged classic "hard sell" techniques practiced by army recruiters, although in reality both recruitment techniques existed simultaneously, especially at the VAE. Both venues, as explicit public recruitment endeavors, generated considerable national attention and media coverage that often focused on protests that were regularly held at both. While the voices of these protesters are, I think, important to consider, in this chapter I also turn my attention to those individuals who worked at both the VAE and the AEC. I examine their own points of view in regards to their labor in the name of army recruitment.

This special focus on those people who work within the production environment of militarized gaming media attributes agency to those involved in both the production and the consumption of militarized media. In doing so I seek to avoid positioning the only possibilities of gamer subjectivity along dualistic lines wherein one must be either a "media activist" and vocal dissenter against militarized games or a "media dupe" who passively buys into all of the militarized messages within games. This approach stems from my personal understanding of the pleasures and problematics of militarized games and reflects my discovery of a nuanced and thoughtful critical reflection that is already present among those who actually engage with and produce such media on a daily basis.

Many of the people whose views I detail below actively contributed through their work to the militarization of popular culture. But the complexities of ethnographic experience have made it imperative for me to include the thoughtful yet ambiguous voices I have found over the course of my research. These points of view complicate the common knee-jerk "for or against" political mentality that often emerges among even thoughtful academics and other individuals when polarizing issues such as military recruitment are discussed. Divergent individual and institutional interpretations regarding the meanings of Army Game Project products were apparent among even its employees, who continually reinscribed the game and franchise with new meanings that were divergent from, but not necessarily contradictory to, the official army message.

From Air Shows and State Fairs . . .

At the time when Russia was invading the post-Soviet nation of Georgia and the 2008 Beijing Olympics were being broadcast worldwide, the vae was making a prolonged two-week stay in Indiana during the Indiana State Fair and the Indianapolis Air Show. On my way there, as I blearily stood in the Atlanta airport after a grueling cross-country red-eye flight, a soldier in the Army National Guard limped to the front of the line, everyone's sleepy eyes fixed on the back of his head. He was in full uniform with a pack on his shoulder, wore a neck brace, and used a cane to walk. I wondered whether, like Rieman's Real Hero backstory, this returning injured soldier was a darker face of a multimedia Janus.

The Virtual Army Experience sat at the Indiana State Fair among the General Motors and Saturn tents, a trailer promoting biofuels, and the fairground's 4-H building. Its physical shell, part tractor-trailer and part inflatable structure, was visible across most of the fairground. Huge fans in the back of the structure had to constantly be kept blowing lest the entire thing collapse. The vae came in four sizes, each named according to army unit designations: Alpha, Bravo, Charlie, and Delta. These configurations traveled across the country, predominantly to events in more populous areas that have traditionally served as a base for army recruitment, such as the South, the Midwest, and the Southwest. Alpha was the largest configuration (holding up to forty people) and Delta the smallest (accommodating only about five people at a time), but Bravo and Charlie (which held between fifteen and twenty people each) were the most typical versions, each collapsing to fit within three full-size tractor-trailers. Alpha was essentially a combination of Bravo and Charlie, and when these two configurations came together at events such as the Indianapolis Air Show a huge interior space was fashioned.

An executive developer of the VAE, Mark Long,[3] described the interior of the multimedia experience to me in terms that emphasized the functional integration between digital and physical elements. The featured highlights of the VAE were mock-up Humvees and Black Hawk helicopters, the movement of which was simulated through 180-degree screens and

> kinetic hammers that, when an explosion goes off, rock the Humvee [see fig. 10]. And gas action weighted recoil mechanisms on the weapons. So you get this kinetic integration. You know, when you're trying to physically control the muzzle climb on a weapon, shooting in a simulation allows you to suspend disbelief more. Suddenly that physical integration into the virtual environment takes you in and creates a greater sense of presence, which is really cool. And then there are air cannons and audio, the whole thing. So it's a lot of fun. They have two of these systems and they bring them around to air shows and NASCAR, and men [who visit] there—young men and women—they can give their email address and then go through and try it, and a recruiter can follow up to see if there's any interest. You don't really decide to join the army because you went through the VAE. But you get to try something cool with your friends for about five minutes and you give up your email address for it, so it seems like a fair deal.

In the following account, I describe a typical experience of the VAE, which I composited over the course of my fieldwork at the venue. I typically attended one or two full VAE sequences each day, and hung around the venue at other times for several hours, talking with participants and interviewing and chatting with employees and soldiers, all of whom were aware of my presence there as a researcher.

Press releases and advertisements typically emphasized the interior simulation of the VAE containing the Humvees, and brought attention to the virtuality of the experience, going so far as to claim that the VAE is a "test drive" of army enlistment. For example, within the Alpha VAE structure visitors were able to get "a virtual test drive of the United States Army. The core of the 9,750-square-foot VAE is the *America's Army* computer game, rendered with state-of-the-art Army training simulation technology to create a life-size, networked virtual world. The VAE highlights key Soldier occupations, Army technologies, operating environments and missions, within a fast-paced, action-packed, information-rich experience that immerses visitors in the world of Soldiering. Participants employ teamwork, rules of engagement, leadership and high-tech equipment as they take part in a virtual U.S. Army mission" (Army Game Project 2007).

In fact, most visitors spent a significant amount of the time outside the actual simulation. The wait outside was often as short as twenty minutes, but was reportedly as long as four hours, with the typical length of time spent inside the VAE being thirty to forty minutes. To help participants kill some time during the wait, army recruiters and drill sergeants stood around, ready to chat with people about the army or give away army T-shirts, hats, and copies of the *America's Army* Xbox video game to people who did enough proper push-ups (see fig. 11).

A representative from the army-sponsored Top Fuel dragster racing team was there as well, taking complimentary photos of anyone who wished to have their picture taken with the car. This was a popular option for kids who could not enter the VAE, as the posted minimum age was thirteen years old.[4] Near the building videos explained the fourfold process of registering, obtaining the mission briefing, playing the simulation, and participating in the after-action review. Video teasers for the VAE played repetitively on larger screens on top of the trailers.[5]

After the wait in the heat outside, visitors entered the air-conditioned registration lobby, where they were greeted by several locally hired young women standing behind a counter and computers. They asked everyone a series of required questions: "Are you interested in learning about the army?" "Have you or your family ever served in a branch of the military?" They also collected more basic information from individuals, such as their addresses, telephone numbers, email addresses, and levels of education. They took each visitor's photo and presented each with a Virtual Army Experience ID card, which fit inside a neck wallet equipped with an RFID sensor that tracked each person's movement within the VAE. All of this information was collated by a subcontractor, Fish Software (now called simply FISH), to produce a large database of demographic information that aided in producing knowledge about the effectiveness of particular displays within the VAE and the efficiency of national venues in garnering a population of potential recruits. Information was also transferred to local recruiters, as I personally discovered when a Seattle-based army recruiter later followed up, cold calling me two days after I truthfully indicated at registration in Indianapolis that I was "interested in learning more about the army."

As people waited for everyone in their group to finish with the registration process, visitors were able to kill some time by playing *America's Army* at computer stations in the center of the room. For most this was their first time playing the game, and most of the time visitors spent playing was devoted simply to learning the basic interface of the controllers. Once everyone in the group was registered, a man introduced himself to the group as a subject matter expert (SME). He invited everyone to stand in line as a group and explained the weapon systems simulated inside the VAE, such as the Black Hawk helicopter and Humvees mounted with CROWS (Common Remotely Operated Weapons System), which use controller interfaces similar to video game joysticks (Pappalardo 2010). The SME told the group that he served in the army in Iraq, and that anyone with questions about the VAE or the army should ask him at any time. He then opened a door leading to the interior of the VAE and a huge, dark space filled with life-size mock-ups of Humvees and a Black Hawk helicopter.

Before people could take their seats inside these vehicles, however, the SME directed everyone to watch a five-minute video in which the group—now referred to as a "squad"—was briefed on the upcoming mission. In this video a colonel and several officers described the scenario of Nradreg's humanitarian plight (see chapter beginning), using official-sounding, euphemistically unintelligible jargon while conveying the seriousness of the situation through tone and dramatic music. At the end of the video the SME showed the squad a map of the area that displayed critical points of the mission. He then instructed people how to identify civilians, told everyone not to shoot at them, and directed the squad to take a seat in one of the vehicles.

Unlike roller coasters or motion simulations, there was no overall consensus among visitors about which seat or vehicle was best for the experience. Shooting from the Black Hawk helicopter, as opposed to the Humvee, was objectively more difficult. Sometimes SMEs tried to preempt complaints about the Black Hawk being too hard by framing it as a "target practice challenge" in their briefings beforehand. This "are you good enough?" kind of framing typically encouraged younger men to sit in the Black Hawk mock-up. Guns, properly weighted and convincingly real, were mounted to the vehicles (see fig. 10), and the M249 SAW turret guns at the tops of the Humvees tended to be popular. After standing in line for over half an hour, though, many chose instead to sit in the Humvees. This, I contend, is one of the microlevel purposes of the VAE: to introduce the army's technologies and weapons systems to the general public so that civilians would, for instance, be able to make a more informed decision as to which vehicle or which seat in a U.S. Army Humvee is more appropriate for them to ride in. In the minutiae of such options and necessary decisions virtual soldiers are thus fashioned.

After the simulation began squad members were able to fire the air rifles mounted on the vehicles. At this point there were no targets, and a montage of scenes accompanied by heavy-metal music appeared on the three large screens in front of each vehicle. This sequence showed missiles launching, army helicopters starting their run to the battlefield, and HALO (high altitude low opening) parachutists making their jump. Finally the montage changed to an aerial view that swooped down to the squad's position, and the camera flew into a virtual Humvee, bringing everyone to a first-person perspective as if they were viewing the action from inside their vehicle. Although there was no actual driver the vehicle started moving on-screen, accompanied by a physical rumbling from the vehicle that simulated movement. The screens showed civilians running away, and, although the SME told visitors not to shoot at them, some (sometimes including me) usually did anyway, often out of boredom. The virtual civilians, however, did not react in any way and kept on running. If visitors persisted in shooting at civilians, the SME threatened to remove them from the simulation.

Shortly, however, several men with guns ran out, crouched in the middle of the road, and started firing their weapons in what appeared to be the direction of the vehicles. The squad swiftly took them out, but soon afterward an enemy jeep drove up. After taking just a few bullets the jeep exploded, creating a vibration felt from the seat of the Humvee.

After a few minutes of this, people began to realize that there was nothing the enemy could do that could hurt their virtual selves—that they were a spectator to the action rather than an active agent in a game. This, at least, was my feeling once I realized I was not playing a game with the potential to lose, but was instead fighting a pushover enemy that was going to let me win no matter what. Still, the seven minutes of cinematic target practice went by swiftly, ending with the convoy crossing a bridge and arriving at the refugee camp, thus completing the objective of the mission. Some squad members, including me, tried to shoot the refugees and aid workers, but as nothing happened we sadly realized that our weapons were no longer effective. One visitor, blogging on the technology news website CNET, described a similar experience of the simulation:

> I had fun during the intense but short experience. It felt surprisingly real, with the gun and Humvee shaking and rocking wildly as I shot at terrorists on a huge screen. Unfortunately, it didn't really present the same level of risk most video games offer. As far as I could tell, nobody in the simulation died or got hurt. Sure, bullets flew and bombs exploded, but nobody lost a life and had to respawn, or any other of the typical game conventions you'd expect from an FPS [first-person shooter] or a light-gun game. It was like I was playing through an Army mission in god mode.[6] (Greenwald 2007)

Although some may find the idea of shooting at virtual civilians appalling, I suggest that most people did not do it out of spite or as a result of any "corrupting" influence of video games. Rather, visitors shot at civilians to test the limits of believability in this virtual environment, to push back against and reappropriate in some small way the scripted heroic narrative so thoroughly entrenched and blatantly present at the VAE. The act of shooting at civilians was the most powerful and common mode of speaking back to authority I witnessed inside the VAE. The inability of civilians—or, for that matter, players—to die was disappointing; it punched through the logic of the claim I often heard during my time at the VAE that "this is as close to realistic combat as you can get outside of going to war."[7] John Grant, a member of the antiwar organization Veterans for Peace, equated this kind of experience with "the reality level of that good ol' TV show *The A-Team*, where they'd go out on these special missions and it's like, '*Brrrrummmm! Brmbrmrbmrb-mrm, brrrrrrrrmbrmbrmbrmbrm. Powpow.*' Booooombs! And guuuuuns! And bullets and people flying. Nobody even gets a hangnail, and at the end they're smoking cigars. Everybody's happy and there's not a mark on them. They're all as handsome as they were before. That's exactly the problem—there are no consequences."

As the simulation ended, the SME directed everyone to exit the VAE structure to a small tent, where he conducted an After Action Review in which he showed the squad images he claimed were taken during the game. These images never varied, nor did the essence of the SME's review, which conveyed to the squad that they did a good job but needed to work more on teamwork and communicating with other members in their vehicles. At this point the SME had the group watch another video, this one about an *America's Army* Real Hero.[8] At the conclusion of the video the actual Real Hero entered the tent as the SME introduced him to the group. The Real Hero told the group more about his experiences in the army and handed out a Real Heroes action figure made in his likeness (see fig. 8) to a member of the group, often to the youngest-looking visitor or to an individual who indicated at registration that he or she would be interested in joining the army. He then made himself available to sign autographs or chat about the army with anyone interested. The SME directed people to remove their neck wallets but to keep their VAE ID cards, and as visitors returned their wallets, they were given a copy of the *America's Army* PC game attached to a VAE lanyard. The visitors walked away to the rest of the state fair, perhaps going to the 4-H building or the dog show nearby.

Although the VAE takes its name from the technology of virtual reality, when considering the population of visitors to the VAE, another sense of the word *virtual*—that is, a connotation of potential—is also germane. The visitors to the VAE were virtual soldiers, a force not yet mobilized, and the VAE served as a conduit in actualizing the potential of this labor pool. Fish Software, the contracting company responsible for gathering data on visitors and disseminating them to relevant entities like recruitment offices and OEMA, was forthright about this function of the VAE, explaining that "though the VAE will garner much attention for being a realistic and compelling war simulator, the purpose of it is clear—to collect actionable information that allows the Army to recruit more effectively. Every aspect of the experience is geared toward delivering positive messages about the Army and collecting information that can be leveraged post-event" (Fish Software 2007, 3).

The development, construction, presentation, and post-event aspects of the VAE further involved a constellation of part-time, temporary, and full-time laborers. These too were a virtual army in the sense that they were not a part of the U.S. Army proper but nevertheless fulfilled many of the functions of the army, as contracting entities of the so-called "military entertainment complex." This virtual army was composed of SMEs, technicians, tour directors, public relations representatives (all employees of Ignited), young women staffing registration and checkout (hired on a temporary basis through local modeling agencies), drivers (employees of Performance Marketing Group), and employees of Fish Software, the army-sponsored Top Fuel dragster racing team, and McCann Erikson (the marketing agency responsible for the "Army Strong" campaign). In addition to this virtual army of contractors, enlisted army recruiters, the Real Heroes, and drill sergeants were all involved in the VAE media campaign. The men (mostly nonmilitary or ex-military contractors) who toured with the VAE as production staff, tended to speak of their work as if they were comrades-in-arms in a fashion similar to the *America's Army* game developers (see chapter 6). "You know," one employee told me, "anytime you're on the road it's just like the Band of Brothers in the sense that you go through the worst things on Earth. I mean, obviously we're not in Iraq, but stuff will break and somehow we always make it work. I like that camaraderie."

This virtual army existed to support the continual flow of visitors and the occasional media or VIP visit to the VAE. Although this breakdown admittedly falls into the trap of categorizing individuals based on the type of work they do, it is nevertheless useful in beginning to think about the sheer variety of activities, motivations, interests, organizations, and logistics involved in putting on a production such as the VAE. A step back from this local level of actors reveals even more layers of organizations connected to the VAE. Zombie Studios, the *America's Army* California studios, the SED at Redstone Arsenal, and OEMA are only the most central organizations in a complex array of institutions that had a hand in the production and implementation of the VAE.

Reducing the VAE to a singular kind of experience or a pithy description of what it did or was is difficult; rather, it communicated a variety of messages through different channels and media, and it did so not simply through a unidirectional form of information dissemination, as in the traditional understanding of propaganda. The experiences of each visitor, of course, varied depending on the individuals present, the venue at which the VAE was presented, the size and configuration of the VAE, and an infinite number of other factors. The army predictably sought to limit variations in visitor interpretations by framing the experience in a highly scripted manner that communicated positive messages to participants, especially teenagers, about the career opportunities available in the army. It did this not only through multiple videos, but also through use of *America's Army*, the VAE simulation, and (usually) charismatic recruiters, drill sergeants, Real Heroes like Tommy Rieman, and SMEs. Brian, one of the VAE's production staff, explained that this effort to humanize the army was very intentional because

> traditional media marketing efforts for the army—they have always come off as being sort of half-assed and really goofy. You see television commercials and the things that they really hype up are things like "honor" and "duty" and stuff, and it falls flat, I think. It's just images and audio. [The VAE] really puts a human face on things whereas on a TV commercial nine times out of ten you are seeing actors and it's really insincere, really uninteresting, and really unengaging. Even in *America's Army* you can go into a Virtual Recruiting Center to meet the Real Heroes [simulated in the game] and learn about their stories. They're real people, but so much of army advertising is not even virtual but artificial.

The scripted stories of the Real Heroes were at the center of the *America's Army* campaign to place a human face on the army and directly challenged absurdly unrealistic advertising orientations such as the one described by Marcus in the epigraph to this chapter. Both Marcus and Brian, however, also understood that the interpretative framing surrounding *America's Army* and such related venues as the VAE and the

AEC was also thoroughly constructed since they had had a hand in producing the interpretive material.

The VAE framed the actual appearance of the Real Hero near the end of the public tour as the most significant interpretative moment of the experience (see fig. 12). Carefully chosen as representatives who present a realistic career goal for prospective recruits (with seven enlisted soldiers or noncommissioned officers and two commissioned officers), the Real Heroes were portrayed as ordinary soldiers who, through their training in the army, became enabled to do heroic deeds. As one Real Hero put it, "none of us were trying to be heroes, we were just there doing our job."[9] Another states, "I don't see myself as a hero. I just see myself as Tommy Rieman, doing my job. I think everybody has the same quality, but they just have to find it."[10]

SMES (subject matter experts) also played a significant role in personalizing the army at the VAE and were central to interpreting the VAE to visitors in a way that attempted to maximize the number of people leaving with a more favorable impression of the army. Some SMES cracked jokes and kept their explanations upbeat, while others chose to focus on describing their own experiences and career trajectories that enlistment in the army allowed. One SME, for example, informed visitors about his deployments and return, but chose to tell visitors mostly about his subsequent pursuit of a college degree with army support. SMES said their job was to "educate, promote, and entertain the public," and they conceptualized their work as both performer and educator. "I think I'm a little bit of each," one SME told me,

> because I like making people smile and have a good time because that's what this is about. It's not about trying to impress people or make them think they're in the army. I like to entertain them, because the army isn't that bad. A lot of people are like, "Oh, if I join the military I'm going to get shot at," and all this kind of stuff, but no, it depends on what job you do. I try to educate people and [tell them], "No, you could be a satellite technician, and do three or four years, get out, make over a hundred grand a year with your military education and experience." So, educate. And then, I might crack a few jokes [. . .] and just try to make good laughs and have a good time.

SMES were all former enlistees in the army, and many worked as contract employees at the VAE between stints of active duty. As such the SMES themselves blurred the lines between soldier and civilian, and stood in as the most visible mechanism of the "soft sell" at work at the VAE. As contractors who sold their labor to the military as both enlisted and civilian employees, the SMES embodied post-Fordist virtual soldiering. Brian explained this to me in his own way, rhetorically asking,

> What is the product that the VAE wants to punch out? On one level you have the game that we give away, but at the end of the day, it's all about recruiting. What's the product, though? The Real Heroes are sort of the cream of the crop; they are the ultimate product. But I think on a larger scale you have to look at the subject matter experts. I think that those guys who were just regular folks in the army—some did combat, some didn't—I think that those are the real products. Those guys are literally 'products' of the army.

Although the VAE was a marketing effort to sell a real experience of joining and being in the U.S. Army, there were a plethora of other "products"—both literal and metaphorical—that shaped a visitor's experience at the VAE. The SMES, army recruiters, and Real Heroes (all "products" of the army) helped create and sustain a militarized, highly masculine, and scripted experience that guests were able to take home with them after their visit (cf. Kline et al. 2003, 247–68; Enloe 2000). Items given to visitors (ID cards, key chains, action figures, T-shirts, hats, and video games) were some of these take-home products, as were the intangible memories of the experience. Additionally, people who fit the right demographic and who indicated an interest in the army also took home with them the prospect of being contacted in the near future by a local army recruiter.

As the finely tuned military stories and experiences present at the VAE demonstrate, there was a carefully executed deployment of persuasive technologies at work here. The Army Experience Center, the stationary cousin of the Virtual Army Experience, brought these technologies, narratives, and simulated experiences together in an unparalleled manner to intermesh militarized forms of entertainment, education, business, and public service—all in the name of U.S. Army recruitment.

Ignited took its concept of the Virtual Army Experience and expanded it, in association with entities at the Pentagon,[11] to create the Army Experience Center, which sat at the far end of the winding Franklin Mills Mall in Philadelphia, Pennsylvania, surrounded by an indoor skateboard park, a video game arcade, a Chinese restaurant, Banana Republic, and Victoria's Secret. Although the AEC was not a formal part of the Army Game Project and therefore not under the supervision of OEMA and Wardynski, it was closely connected due the fact that it was also managed by Ignited, and maintained many formal and informal relationships with Army Game Project institutions. As a related Pentagon-supervised program that used both *America's Army* software and the same VAE Humvee and Black Hawk simulators, the AEC arguably generated more contention and news coverage than either, with reports from CNN, NBC *Nightly News*, and the *New York Times*, as well as independent media organizations, activist organizations, and PBS.[12] Public relations representatives from Ignited with whom I spoke were generally happy with this wide exposure, claiming that "in the last two years we've maintained 97 percent positive to neutral coverage."[13]

Like the VAE and *America's Army*, the AEC was designed to appeal primarily to teenage boys, yet the center had a vibe that was meant to be welcoming to anyone wishing know more about the army, or simply wishing to relax from shopping, watch TV, or play video games. Civilian staff and army recruiters typically kept a courteous distance from visitors unless they were approached. Their dress was casual, with uniforms of khaki pants with white or black army polo shirts or jackets, color-coded to distinguish soldiers from civilians. As the AEC's director Al Flood explained to me, "We're here to have the space for people to learn about the army in their own way." The center contained big-screen televisions, anchored to the ceiling, playing ESPN and other programs in closed captioning, and plush sofas and chairs were arranged in clusters behind the front registration desk. Several interactive kiosks featured additional information on various army military occupational specialties (MOSES), global base locations, starting soldier salaries, and salary projections based on experience, education, and rank. A small area displayed army merchandise available for purchase. To one side was a regularly used classroom with approximately forty computers and seats, referred to as the "Tactical Operations Center" and visible through transparent glass walls.

Further back were four rows of seats with sixty desktop computers (see fig. 13) and nineteen Xbox 360 consoles with plush seats along the wall. These were available for anyone over the age of thirteen to walk in and use, on the condition that they enter their personal contact information in a database at the front registration desk and provide proof of age and identity. (Games rated "Mature" on the ESRB scale were off limits to users under the age of seventeen. This excluded most first-person shooting games besides *America's Army*, which was deliberately rated "Teen.") Once visitors registered they obtained an official AEC card and number, which enabled information on individual users to be stored for statistical tracking and demographic analysis. In the very back of the center were Apache helicopter and Humvee simulators identical to those at the VAE. The center's recruiting and management offices, visible through large glass walls, were located behind doors.

The aura of transparency was important at the AEC, both metaphorically and literally. Taking pains to exude as casual an atmosphere as possible, and with an abundance of glass windows in its interior and on all sides facing the mall corridors to visually represent transparency in army recruiting, the AEC epitomized the military recruitment soft sell in perhaps its purest form to date. This two-year, $13 million experimental pilot program, which lasted from August 2008 to July 2010, combined five Philadelphia-area recruiting stations into one. Twenty civilian staff and twenty-two enlisted army recruiters—handpicked from recruiting school by the Center's Pentagon project manager, Major Larry Dillard—replaced forty regular army recruiters. "It's an overall change in philosophy" in recruiting, Dillard told me, and while people at the Pentagon were quick to recognize the potential of the center to revolutionize army recruiting strategies, recruiters entrenched in the system of the hard sell and the cold call were often less willing to change.

I was told that one of the primary reasons for locating the AEC in the Philadelphia area was that army demographic research had indicated that approximately one third of all army recruits came from within a fifty-nautical-mile radius of an existing army base. This, combined with the fact that the army has traditionally garnered low recruiting numbers from urban areas, led to the consideration of sites in Baltimore, Albuquerque, Fresno, Chicago, and Philadelphia as possible locations for the AEC. The Franklin Mills Mall was eventually chosen for its access to public transportation as well as the ethnic and class diversity of its shoppers. Locations like Philadelphia's King of Prussia Mall, where "everyone is rich and preppy," and other malls that "aren't as nice," were ruled out.[14]

Though recruiting was, by all measures, an end goal at the AEC, as a pilot project the center integrated data collection goals for market research, in addition to an overarching goal of repositioning the army as a "community-building" organization. The data collection portion of the AEC's mission was often left unsaid or implied by its representatives, though it arguably constituted the most important part of the AEC's activities in terms of long-term proof-of-concept measuring and budgeting for future AEC-like projects. Unless a person provided specific permission during registration, personal information was not used to contact individuals for the purposes of recruitment. Instead, information was collected for demographic mapping of the sets of interests that various groups of visitors brought to the AEC. Each visitor who logged on to a computer was required to complete a set of several simple questions, composed by Wardynski himself, for the purposes of collecting "actionable information." This information was collected and analyzed for marketing and event planning at the AEC and for "learn[ing] more about how the army may further adapt technology to harness the power of the information age to support the recruiting mission" (U.S. Congress 2010, 318). In the event that the soft sell proved to be an effective and desirable strategy for military recruitment, this corpus of data was intended to be leveraged in the design of future, more permanent Army Experience Centers across the United States.

In addition to these long-term goals for setting up additional AECs nationwide—goals that have yet to be realized—the most commonly stated goals of the AEC by its representatives involved "community building." This was not mere rhetoric, either, but instead a central component of an emerging strategy of rebranding the U.S. Army to the American public as a constructive, rather than destructive, social force that provides positive "opportunities" for individuals and groups. Al Flood, the

AEC's Ignited director, explained these twin recruitment and "community building" goals of the AEC by stating that "our mission here is to make people in the area, number one, aware of their army and in particular of the active duty army. And also to really increase their awareness of the opportunities that exist in the army. Career opportunities, educational opportunities. [. . .] If people walk in here and they leave, if nothing else, with having a better appreciation of what the army does and for what the people in the army do and the sacrifices they make— mission accomplished."

One of the most noteworthy aspects of the AEC that I witnessed during my on-site fieldwork there, and afterward through my continued engagement with the center through its email updates and online presence, was its capability and willingness to regularly organize well-attended public events that appealed to young adults. While some of these events contained explicit military connections and themes, many of them did not. Some of the major events sponsored and produced by the AEC included monthly movie nights for screening films (e.g., *Blackhawk Down, Twilight: New Moon, Terminator: Salvation, Avatar*); visits from professional athletes (e.g., Philadelphia Phillies 2008 World Series champion pitcher Brad Lidge); regular video game tournaments for a variety of games (e.g., *Call of Duty: World at War, HALO 3 ODST, Madden NFL '10*); three-on-three basketball tournaments; a Christmas and a "Christmas in July" charity clothing drive; a Halloween *Thriller* dance party that was an attempt to break a national record for the greatest number of simultaneous *Thriller* dancers; and the sponsorship of Philadelphia School District–wide events such as the Asian/Pacific Islander Heritage Month Senior Leadership Forum, and similar events during Black History Month in February and Women's History Month in March.

Something clearly was at work at the AEC beyond (stereo)typical "hard sell" army recruitment efforts, which are usually concerned with meeting quotas and filling seats for basic training. Beatrice Jauregui (2015) describes articulations made by "community-building" programs and venues such as the AEC as manifestations of a shift in focus of the army's conceptualizations of soldier "fitness." This pseudoholistic model of soldier fitness extends beyond soldiers themselves, situating soldier families and the broader "community" as subjects of army programs. Such programs, specifically the AEC and the Comprehensive Soldier Fitness program (launched in 2009), articulate a desire on the part of the army "to demonstrate that it creates good citizens as moral subjects, not only by putting them through the soldier-making machine, but also by entreating them to share their strength through direct and routinized interactions with the community" (Jauregui 2015, 18–19).

In operationalizing "the community" in this way, the AEC successfully partnered with schools, and AEC management actively worked to foster relationships with Philadelphia-area public schools and teachers. "We've been here long enough that high schools and high school teachers now contact us to come here for class trips," Flood declared. Reserving the AEC for school events was a simple matter, possible through the center's website. Free transportation to and from the AEC, along with event planning, was a simple process arranged by the on-site AEC events coordinator. Flood explained to me that these were part of

> a long-term effort to get partnerships with educational outreach organizations, community outreach organizations. We've also tied in with a separate nonprofit to—believe it or not—conduct high school–level culinary arts competitions to simply showcase the high school students who are participating in [alternative high school] programs. [This] allows us to showcase their achievements and a path to a potential future career that they've already started on. But it also allows us the opportunity to bring in a member of the United States Army culinary arts team and say, "Hey, did you know that you could be a master chef in the army?" "What? That's crazy!" "No, it's not!" We have actual master chefs in the army, so ultimately the message we send is, "Hey high school students, you're doing great—keep it up. Continue to do what you're doing. Make smart life decisions."

This kind of contextual framing of events for high school students positions army enlistment as being the smartest life decision possible, especially for the mostly underprivileged youth who were already participating in AEC-sponsored educational programs. Further emphasizing such "life opportunities," the AEC partnered with PHASE 4 Learning Center, an alternative high school program, to host daily high school courses taught within the AEC's networked and sleek Tactical Operations Center.

During my on-site fieldwork there, the majority of guests present at the AEC during working hours on weekdays were PHASE 4 high school students, taking classes and using technology made available to them by the army. PHASE 4 recognizes the precariousness of many of their students, and its funders indicate that many come from low-income families.[15] Given this embeddedness of PHASE 4 within the AEC, it is not surprising that a higher-than-average rate of 10 percent of graduating PHASE 4 students planned to undertake military service.[16]

After the AEC finished its two years of operation, its director Al Flood also transitioned to become the PHASE 4 regional vice president for the Philadelphia area. Given these and other explicit military connections,[17] it is difficult *not* to see the partnerships between the AEC and educational institutions as being an unambiguous conduit for guiding at-risk youth toward the military. Just as the distinction between the civilian and soldier is at least temporarily eroded and deemphasized at the AEC, the transition between these educational and soldierly spheres of experience is made easy and almost commonsensical by the institutional relationships that are fostered between the AEC, schools, and community organizations.

The educational partnerships at the AEC are framed as "life opportunities" that transition individuals along a path of career success toward an optimistic future, but at their core these relationships between the army and "the community" deliberately exploit a class and racial system of structural inequalities, which provides few attractive alternatives for employment or advancement besides military service to low-income youth of color. In this sense the AEC is a clear manifestation of Deleuze's control societies, in which "the family, the school, the army, the factory are no longer distinct analogical spaces" (1992, 6). The formation of military subjects—militarization—no longer happens only at the military base or on the battlefield (wherever that may be), but now happens across institutions and in less institutionalized settings such as state fairs, air shows, *Thriller* dance parties, and three-on-three basketball tournaments. Managing the AEC, Al Flood told me, "is kind of like owning the first McDonald's, or working at the first McDonald's. You know it's going to be an amazing thing, but you know some days are going to be really, really hard and other days are not." Later, after the AEC hosted an "Asian/Pacific Islander Heritage Month Senior Leadership Forum" for local high school students, I overheard Flood ask an army recruiter, "How did the lunch line go today?" The recruiter replied, "We need more turkey, less ham, no wraps" (see fig. 14).

Militarization is a process of subject formation that is no longer unidirectional and originating solely from a monolithic military state power, but one that is cybernetic—performed and incorporative of the feedback of its militarized subjects. This means that the participation of "the community" is a critical component of processes of militarization in the twenty-first century. This also means that even those who seek to oppose militarizing tendencies sometimes cannot escape its logics.

Critics and Protesters

The vae and aec were both lightning-rod venues that drew significant crowds of protesters. Part of the reason for the vehemence of protest stemmed from a perceived trivialization of war through its representation in a digital, game-like context. "War is not a game," was an often-repeated phrase during these protest events, which were well attended (and often organized) by members of the organization Veterans for Peace and allied antiwar groups. For example, a representative from Veterans for Peace declared in a public statement that "massacring people on a screen I don't think is good for young people. It gives a distorted message about what the Army is doing today." Another representative added, "We don't want to come across as criticizing the Army. Many of us have seen combat and have been decorated. But this thing uses violence to seduce young people into enjoying a very false depiction of war" (O'Malley 2008). Such strong reactions were bound up in an array of issues stretching beyond the strong antiwar stance of Veterans for Peace. They stemmed in part from a profound fear and misunderstanding of the emergent medium of video games, a fear that has historically accompanied the emergence of other new media such as television and radio (Jenkins 2004, 2005).

At both the aec and vae protest organizations like Veterans for Peace took on a militarized logic of their own by privileging the experiences of former soldiers as being a more valid basis upon which antiwar protest might be organized.[18] Brian, a vae employee, saw a certain level of disingenuousness in the justifications of protesters, asserting to me that so much of society—American society specifically—is incredibly militarized, but we don't see it. You can hang out and watch the History Channel and that might not bother you, but it's all basically war. You could write a whole thesis on sports and militarization in the United States, but for some reason [we don't see it]. For example, the VAE goes to a lot of air shows, and air shows to me have always been military stuff, where you're flexing your military muscle, you're showing off these machines that are designed to murder people, basically. And that's fine if you want to boil it down to that. But what's interesting is that at the Cleveland Air Show every year we have a group of protesters [who are mostly military veterans] that is very anti-VAE. They're really confused, though, in the sense that they'll say that the air show is just "a celebration of American aviation," but what we're doing [at the VAE] is so indicative of the militarization of American culture and how bad [the United States is] going down like Rome. They don't see it, it's like the forest from the trees thing. America is completely militarized in so many ways, but so is most of Western culture. It's so easy to find something like the VAE and put your thumb on it, but it's such a bigger societal issue than just the VAE. [. . .] I think with protesters like that, to go after something really big like this is the easy way out—to say that this is big and evil and it's going to hurt people.

While Brian saw the positions of some protesters as duplicitous, in the sense that the VAE was being singled out at the expense of a broader possible critique of cultural militarization in the United States, other employees at the VAE expressed different kinds of vocal and negative reactions against organized protesters. "I've heard about the horror stories of protesters showing up," a VAE subject matter expert and former soldier told me, "but I really hope I don't have to deal with them. I wouldn't get angry with them, I wouldn't react. I'd let the media people deal with them, but I don't believe that people should protest [the VAE]." Antiwar protest, I was told, was unpatriotic. Notably, this extreme ideological position was articulated only by enlisted or former soldiers. Other SMEs were more even-handed, and asserted that the essence of the problem was in imparting the proper army-mediated interpretation to visitors: "Protesters think this game is here to entice children and make it seem like killing is glamorous, but SMES are here to make sure that it's not interpreted in that way."

Brian, who had no military background, explained to me that this kind of interpretation was exactly how he imagined *America's Army* when he first heard about the game when he was in high school. In his mind's eye he saw "guys in an office manically planning out how they are going to get guys in the army. And after working with [the VAE] and doing it for so long I don't think it's that at all. It's an honest, sincere effort to put people in the army. It's not this sort of Orwellian, vindictive thing where they are just trying to trick people into joining the army, which I think is something that is very easy for people to think. [. . .] In my experience, it's not like that."

This realization, combined with Brian's interest in Noam Chomsky's writings on media, propaganda, and politics (e.g., Herman and Chomsky 2002) created a lot of "cognitive dissonance" for him in his line of work. "You know," he told me, "I had this super left-wing newspaper that I ran for a long time in college, and I never thought in a million years that I would be working for the army in any capacity, let alone promoting it in this way." Brian spoke candidly about how he

> was thinking about what Chomsky would think about something like [the VAE]. I think it's almost arguable that if he were sitting here, he would say that my reaction to it now is exactly why it works so well— because it doesn't bother me anymore. And that's where propaganda actually works. [The VAE] is propaganda, but so is that Chevy display over there [across from the VAE at the Indiana State Fair]. Propaganda used to not be a bad word until it got associated with Nazism. So pro- paganda is propaganda and the army is just as much a corporation as any other entity out here—that's why it is always at events like this [state fair].

Here Brian equates contemporary corporate marketing with military marketing, calling both forms of "propaganda." This underscores how the corporate, military, and other institutional sectors appear to be increasingly overlapping. While "propaganda" might have negative con- notations if associated with the military, Brian implied, it is not quite so bad if similar marketing methods are used simply to sell products to consumers in a commercial context. Brian was not particularly disturbed by what he saw as being the selling of the army brand—"just as much a corporation as any other entity out there"—at venues like the VAE and the AEC.

Although "propaganda" and "recruitment tool" were explicitly avoided phrasings by the marketing teams for *America's Army*, the VAE, and the AEC, employees readily admitted that their products could be interpreted as being such, including Wardynski himself (Chaplin and Ruby 2005, 219). One *America's Army* producer acknowledged to me that "one person's 'messaging,' of course, is another person's 'propaganda.'" However I use the term "propaganda" with caution and highlight it here simply because it was part of a variety of indigenous, colloquial explanations articulated by employees of the Army Game Project regarding how they viewed *America's Army* and its franchise products. Several, like Brian, were forthright in their opinion that what they were doing was, in some form, the production of propaganda.

Brian's reflexivity concerning his position within the Army Game Project was a complex one that can become lost in the polarizing news reports and academic criticisms that pit the military against protesters and the processes of militarization against critical reflection concerning those processes. A comment made by an Ignited employee during a brainstorming session for the Army Experience Center media outreach plans that "we need to co-op and enlist the anti-recruiting movement to become a part of our movement" indicates that critical reflection sans outright opposition, such as that exhibited by Brian, might be precisely the goal of the soft sell.

For this reason I think that the interpretations of protesters at the VAE and the AEC were grounded in legitimate concerns, which became obfuscated through their consistent vilification of video games as a medium. When I met John Grant, a Vietnam veteran, journalist, and activist in Philadelphia against the AEC, he expressed to me his concern that "these pawns, these kids, need some alternative information. A lot of people in the movement say, 'Oh, we're going to go to the Army Experience Center and we're going to shut it down, shut it down!' Well, I'm more realistic. It's an asymmetrical battle. I don't think we're going to shut it down, at least not today." Grant believed the Army Experience Center was a more insidious venue worthy of protest not because of its use of digital games, but rather because it is "ratcheted up" and has "reached another level" in terms of corporate branding. Like Brian, he also equated the kind of marketing being done at the AEC and VAE as essentially the commercial selling of a product (i.e., army enlistment). Unlike Brian, however, he was particularly disturbed by it: "It's brand selling; it's Disney. It's selling militarism, the myth of militarism, the whole drive of militarism in the form of the brand of the army. It's larger than just recruiting for the army. It's, you know, next to Victoria's Secret in the mall. It's a part of culture. You link it with entertainment, and it becomes something else."

While the U.S. Army has consistently branded itself to potential recruits through previous TV advertising and recruiting campaigns, the explicit and unabashed coupling of the military to corporate "community-oriented" branding evident at the AEC was, for Grant, something newly emergent and alarming. The army was overstepping its institutionally delimited boundaries, ever more fluid and porous in the control societies. Grant understood a critical need for alternative messaging formats and recounted to me his idea to set up "next to the AEC something called the 'Peace Experience Center.'" His concept was uncannily analogous to the real experiences recounted to me earlier by Tommy Rieman, and it perhaps reflected some of his own post-Vietnam experiences as a returning soldier:

> JOHN GRANT: One game I [had an idea for] is a day in the life of a PTSD Iraq vet. He's going to school, and a cop gives him a ticket for his vehicle inspection being overdue—the "fleas of life," as Samuel Beckett called it, that everybody goes through. [It focuses on] some poor kid who's been sent to Iraq or Afghanistan and who is going through all these horrendous things. We know the whole history of post-traumatic stress and repeated tours. What's it like to go through a day [for him after returning home]? And a video game would be perfect . . . The possibilities are endless about the game that you could do to educate a kid as to the realities of what it is like.

ROBERTSON ALLEN: The military is actually making PTSD games [to help rehabilitate] PTSD victims [see Allen 2015; Halpern 2008; McLay 2012].

JG: They are? Interesting. Well, obviously, why not? It's like the psychiatrists they have in Iraq and in places—which is good, I'm not saying it is bad—but they're like the industrial psychologists on the line of a Ford plant or something. The point is to get you back on the line, [. . .] not to address all of the problems that you really have, which is part of being on that goddamn line in the first place.

Grant's comments highlight with mordant irony how games and simulations now participate as an active agent in the recruitment, training, and rehabilitation of soldiers, and are present at every level in soldiers' life-cycle experiences as critical elements in structuring the labor of post-Fordist war. My fieldwork also reveals that the deployment of video game technology for military recruitment purposes is not without ironic moments, as when I witnessed army recruiters encouraging teenagers to play *Guitar Hero* to Rage Against the Machine's song "Killing in the Name" on the Xbox 360 out of the back of a Hummer parked in front of the VAE.[19] The song's concluding mantra ("Fuck you, I won't do what you tell me!"), censored for the game, is Zack de la Rocha's powerful and emotional retort to institutional state power and violence. Indeed, much of the video game industry thrives and profits from the commoditization of irony, a new tactic of the soft sell. If anything, these moments indicate that the military's appropriation of games will continue to be a nexus for continuing important conversations about the consumption of war, the recruitment for the labor of war, and the role of digital technologies in the perpetuation of virtual soldiering.

5 Complicating the Military Entertainment Complex

The theorists of the new U.S. empire have not focused on two important aspects of the institutions that produce its military power: their diversity and complexity and their incompetence and inadequacy to the tasks given them. . . . [D]espite the perception that the military is unified and coherent, its projects are and long have been often as plural, political, and contested as the projects of other arms of the state.

CATHERINE LUTZ, "Empire Is in the Details"

I have this theory: You show me a functional family and I'll show you a family that's hiding something really well.

ERICH IVEANS, [Dev]Pye, former *America's Army* producer, personal interview

Origin Stories

On the other side of the continent from the AEC in my travels to the various organizations connected to the Army Game Project, I found myself leading an impromptu discussion at a long conference table in Los Angeles, surrounded by several men whom I had just met who performed central roles in the design and implementation of both the AEC and the VAE. All were employees of Ignited, the marketing agency for *America's Army*. "I'm sure you've heard the story of Colonel Wardynski," one was telling me, "who saw his sons playing video games and thought that it was a much better venue to start speaking to the youth of America. So he went and banged on a lot of doors to get funding for the program and was eventually able to get the funding to create the game itself, which debuted at E3 [the Electronic Entertainment Expo] in 2002. It was a phenomenal success; everybody thought that because it was coming from the army it was going to be cheap." Like Athena springing from Zeus's head, *America's Army* comes packaged and fully developed in this origin story, the product of an extraordinary individual who, through his innovation and unrelenting determination, singlehandedly conceived and produced his breakthrough product through sheer force of mental will.

This fable was often repeated in multiple versions, as the oral and written mythology of the project proliferated across multiple institutional, personal, and literary channels. Roger Stahl, for example, writes that *"America's Army* is the brainchild of Lt. Col. Casey Wardynski . . . who hatched the idea in 1999, the year when recruitment hit a low mark. Wardynski recognized both the significance of video games in his own sons' lives and the need to tap the market for technologically savvy recruits" (2010, 109). Zhan Li and Tim Lenoir also separately call it Wardynski's "brainchild" (see Lenoir 2008; Li 2003, 12). Phillip Bossant, former art director and executive producer of the game, noted that "Colonel Wardynski recognized and had his own epiphany that appealing to the young means that you have to appeal to the young in ways [with which] they are familiar." Heather Chaplin and Aaron Ruby likewise write, "In 1999 . . . Colonel Wardynski had an epiphany" (2004, 214). Mark Long, former CEO of Army Game Project subcontractor Zombie Studios, called Wardynski "a real maverick in the Pentagon. He's a total outside-the-box thinker and an economist so he has a [. . .] great engineering sensibility but at the same time is deeply practical. And when he first proposed that the army take some tiny fraction of their huge recruiting budget and make a video game out of it I'm sure it was like, are you insane? But it turned out to be the best money they've ever spent. It made the army more relevant and more modern to recruits."

Though these statements are certainly truthful, they underscore the influence and power of an individual at the expense of both historical perspective and the whole constellation of other entities that have contributed to the Army Game Project. They imply that *America's Army* began out of the blue, without precedent. While Wardynski was certainly the single most influential figure in bringing about the *America's Army* franchise and deserves the credit such origin stories give him for envisioning a product and leading it to its completion and evolution, Wardynski is just one person representing one institution within the Army Game Project. Though the project could not have unfolded the way it did without Wardynski's involvement, the connection between the military and gaming was a logical one to make within the U.S. military's evolving cultural milieu of the late nineties and had, in many ways, already been made. *America's Army* is part of a long history of war gaming that stretches back centuries.

The repetitive, similar statements highlighted above regarding Wardynski and *America's Army* point to how this war gaming history has been thoroughly traced and standardized through a variety of academic and journalistic sources, to such an extent that it can be dubbed a *canonical history of war games,* full of obligatory genuflections that highlight through detailed descriptions a series of technologies, institutions, and products that have appeared over the course of the past thirty years and more.[1] Like the origin story of *America's Army*, this canonical history has had a tendency to reproduce a story of deterministic historical progression, to the point in which the history of war games reads nearly the same in all of these texts, regardless of the writer. (To put it in video gaming first-person shooter jargon, this kind of history is "on rails.") Such historical formulations are problematic because they remove a sense of contingency—which is present in all human relationships and organizations—and instead tend to present history as being largely determined through new technologies. In this kind of deterministic history, institutions are presented as being parts of a smooth "network" of interoperable components—individuals, organizations, technologies, and protocols—progressing harmoniously and logically. Individuals move seamlessly in their jobs between companies and organizations, shake hands and make deals, and new technologies just materialize.

Due largely to the work of military think-tank theorists John Arquilla and David Ronfeldt, this "network" metaphor for explaining social and institutional relationships has gained significant clout over the past decade in military circles. Arquilla and Ronfeldt popularized the idea that the U.S. military needs to operate more like a network with substitutable, redundant parts, and less like the hierarchically structured organization that it is (2001). In order to fight effectively a network of terrorist cells, the thinking goes, a conventional military must also operate as if it were a network, with independently acting components that can come to cooperate—or "swarm"—together as a unified whole when necessary, but quickly disseminate back into untraceable, unidentifiable units. The U.S. military has since taken up these tenets of "netwar" theory and applied them to an array of strategic, organizational, and doctrinal procedures, as well as cyberwarfare initiatives (Steele 2001; U.S. Department of the Army 2007).

Critical scholars also drew on the network concept, theorizing the network as a new model for businesses, politics, structures of power, and emergent political movements taking shape in response to these structures of power. In their seminal volume *Empire*, Michael Hardt and Antonio Negri characterize this new model of the network as representing "the passage to the informational economy, [in which] the assembly line has been replaced by the network as the organizational model of production. . . . Production sites can thus be deterritorialized and tend toward a virtual existence, as coordinates in the communication network. As opposed to the old vertical industrial and corporate model, production now tends to be organized in horizontal network enterprises" (2000, 295–96). Such theoretical networks are seamless, virtual, and composed of autonomous nodes working toward a common goal. Such a pure network responds to crisis and incorporates whatever seeks to harm it into its system.

The network concept is important because it has structured how academic writings have couched their descriptions of the military entertainment complex and the canonical history of war games. This includes academic and popular descriptions of *America's Army*, the development of which was a watershed moment in this history of the relationship between entertainment and military sectors in the United States—and indeed globally. While Arquilla and Ronfeldt are themselves careful to take into account the contingent nature of the network, their metaphor has contributed to the prevalence of deterministic top-down explanations of the connections between military and entertainment in the literature. There is utility in this idealized model of a network, but it risks masking how actual, existing networks like the Army Game Project are much more disorganized and potentially prone to failure.

What follows is an attempt to recapture some of the messiness and historical contingencies that are quite often lost in exclusively canonical histories of war gaming, which rely on the language of "the network" and "the military entertainment complex" as shorthand for complex relationships. I draw on some of the oral and written narratives of approximately ten to fifteen (mostly anonymous) game developers, primary and secondary textual sources, and my own ethnographic experience.[2] Like all business endeavors, *America's Army* has always been a project that is very much subject to the individuals and institutions that compose it. At multiple points in its history the project barely survived implosion under the heavy weight of individual rivalries and institutional politics, and the feasibility of the project was very much in doubt. It was never inevitable that *America's Army* would be an initial success, become a franchise enduring more than ten years, or even be published.

A Short History of War Games

War games and simulations are not a new phenomenon, and their modern origins can be traced as least as far as the early nineteenth century. The games chess and *go* are abstract representations of war that have traditionally been given anecdotal authority regarding their efficacy in the visualization of combat, but the modern practice of war gaming had its origins in the game *Kriegsspiel*, which was designed to train officers to envision battles as being constituted by complex but manageable units. Created by a Prussian officer in the aftermath of Napoleon's military ascendancy and eventual defeat, *Kriegsspiel* captured the German public imagination in the mid-nineteenth century, popular both as a leisure activity and military method for understanding war. This mathematical simulation of combat and casualties eliminated from the game many of the contingencies common to actual war, reducing battle to a Malthusian calculus of "cost-benefit analysis" (Halter 2006, 40–46). It proved to be an efficient mode of training, and similar war-gaming practices came to inform the strategies and theory of warfare in other Western European nations and in the United States.

The application and improvement of the kind of war gaming introduced by *Kriegsspiel* continued through the twentieth century and influenced the way the U.S. military and other European states envisioned, planned, and taught war strategy to officers. Nonmilitary populations continued to play war games concurrently as a form of entertainment. H. G. Wells's book *Little Wars: A Game for Boys from Twelve Years of Age to Hundred and Fifty and for That More Intelligent Sort of Girls Who Like Boys' Games and Books* (1913) is essentially a set of rules for playing with toy soldiers, reflecting the deeply masculine and often sexist roots of war gaming that remain to this day.

In the 1950s and 1960s, board-game designers of war games, such as Charles Roberts and James Dunnigan, built on these previously sporadic iterations of war games to develop a full-fledged genre of commercial war gaming that made a general transition from the board game to the computer around the early 1980s. War gaming for entertainment was largely confined to a small group of hobbyists until the commercialization of the home computer, but by the time of Eisenhower's address in 1961 (see chapter 1), aspects of military war gaming had already migrated to the giant and expensive computers that had been built in military-funded research laboratories across the United States.

As a medium of the computer, video games originated from within this military domain. Most video game historians trace the beginnings of the medium back to defense research projects at Brookhaven National Laboratories, MIT, and Stanford in the late 1950s and early 1960s. The commercial industry did not begin growing until the 1970s, with the fabled game *Pong* and Magnavox's Odyssey game system. Atari's dominance during the 1970s and early 1980s—the "Golden Age" of video games—was followed by the North American industry's dramatic crash in 1983, which provided Japanese companies the opportunity for ascendancy in the industry through Nintendo and Sega through the 1980s and early 1990s. For the most part the commercial video game industry and the U.S. military interacted minimally with one another until the 1990s.

Through the ups and downs of the early commercial video game industry, the U.S. military came to more regularly use simulations in the training of specific skills for specialized military roles, such as piloting unique aircraft. SIMNET, the U.S. military's $140 million distributed simulator networking project developed during the mid-1980s and functional by the late-1980s, was a watershed project in its ability to network a huge number of combat units at theater-level operations within an expansive virtual environment that simulated troop movements and combat. Mark Long, who was involved in the production of *America's Army*, recounted how his knowledge and experience with SIMNET contributed to his desire to develop video games and virtual reality technologies. "SIMNET," he told me, "was actually how I got into video games" after leaving the army as a major in 1988:

> Until about 1985–87, simulators were multimillion dollar devices that were one-of-a-kind things built by a small number of companies. And they were really only useful for guys like pilots who had really perishable skills. You can't really practice crashing or ejecting from a plane—you need to have a simulator to do it. But as simulation technology began to get cheaper there was a colonel at DARPA (Defense Advanced Research Projects Agency) who had the idea that you could network them and that these simulators could be valuable to guys who drove tanks, not just airplanes. [. . .] The real value in this system was that it produced collaborative behavior—it wasn't about the quality of the graphics or learning how to engage with the simulator, because they had better simulators for that. It was more intercommunication between the teams and tank crews and that kind of thing. [. . .] And just like *America's Army*, they started adding other systems [. . .] and as early as 1990 you could be in a navy simulator and fly your aircraft off a simulated aircraft deck and land it at an army refueling location. They created this great interoperability. And then the Gulf War happened. This isn't widely known, but a lot of armor officers attributed their unbelievable prowess on the battlefield to the fact that they had run simulations over and over again. They brought SIMNET simulators, in fact, over to Kuwait and these guys built a real database of the desert and were training in that way. And at that point I think the army realized that they had a strategic technology that gave us this enormous advantage. In the early nineties there was a huge growth in simulation.

Long himself was a part of this initial growth in military simulation through the 1980s and 1990s, researching virtual reality technologies at Princeton and the University of Washington, completing military contracting work for *America's Army* and other projects, and securing a $52 million contract from Hasbro to develop a head-mounted device that never went to market.

The 1993 release of *Doom*, the popular first-person shooter (FPS) game that came to define the genre, was a key moment in the contingent relationship between the military and commercial gaming. U.S. Senate hearings on video game violence launched by Joseph Lieberman and Herb Kohl focused on what were then seen as graphic depictions of violence in the game. The in-game violence, which most gamers nowadays would understand as being unrealistically cartoonish, did not bother the U.S. Marines, who by 1997 were using their own ad hoc modifications of *Doom II* to create *Marine Doom*, an unofficial combat simulator. Through the creation of more institutionalized arrangements, a symbiotic relationship between the commercial video game industry and military simulation became more fully realized throughout the 1990s and the following decade, with the private sector driving low-cost technological innovations. The most visible (and canonized) institution symbolizing this relationship is the Institute for Creative Technologies (ICT), designer of the officer combat training simulator *Full Spectrum Warrior*, its commercial Xbox spinoffs, and sequels. The ICT, as a University of Southern California (USC) research institute, draws on expertise in academia, the military, Hollywood, and the gaming industry to produce a variety of experimental technologies for soldier training in "cultural awareness" and PTSD rehabilitation, among other research initiatives.[3]

The groundwork for *America's Army* and multiple venues of cooperation between the Department of Defense and the video game entertainment industry lies in this broader context of the emerging military entertainment complex through the 1990s. A 1997 report generated by the National Research Council's Computer Science and Telecommunications Board entitled *Modeling and Simulation: Linking Entertainment and Defense* (NRC 1997) gave structure to this relationship, which had previously consisted of relatively short-term associations between specific military and commercial entities. This publication detailed future simulation requirements for the Department of Defense and identified ways in which the video game entertainment industry could contribute to the development of these requirements. Games and simulations were deemed important in the report due to their relatively low costs, their ability to handle many users simultaneously for joint training exercises, and their potential affordances for developing both new tactics and weapons systems (NRC 1997, 1).

What the *Modeling and Simulation* report anticipated in 1997 regarding the increased connectivity between the entertainment and defense contracting industry has to a large degree taken place—perhaps partly as a self-fulfilling prophecy. The long-term agenda described in *Modeling and Simulation* articulated military requirements for the development of new technologies that would

a) increase immersion in simulated environments through storytelling and the selective use of sensory details (sight, sound, smell, etc.);
b) provide capabilities for high-speed networks connecting thousands of computers;
c) implement standards for interoperability, enabling different software and hardware programs to work with one another and bypassing proprietary constraints common in media industries;
d) facilitate the quick production and reuse of computer-generated assets in simulations while also developing artificial intelligence that could learn by experience; and
e) provide software and hardware tools to enable the easy production of simulated environments themselves.

Some of these requirements have met with greater success than others. For example capabilities for high-speed networks are no longer a major problem due to the ever-increasing allocation of internet bandwidth, but the implementation of believable artificial intelligence into large-scale training simulations continues to be a difficult, but not insurmountable, issue.

Modeling and Simulation spends a good deal of time discussing the need to overcome the "cultural barriers" (i.e., differences in business practices) between the commercial entertainment industry and the military; this preoccupation is also reflected in other texts from the same era, such that co-written by journalist J. C. Herz and military simulations expert Michael Macedonia (2002). Many of these differences involve issues of production scheduling (typically much longer in military contracting), structures in business models and profit making, long-term research goals, and intellectual property. A key perceived "cultural barrier" highlighted in the report is in the "markedly different objectives" between military and entertainment simulations. "In entertainment the driving actor is excitement and *fun* . . . . Unrealistically dangerous situations, exaggerated hazardous environments, and multiple lives and heroics are acceptable, even desirable, to increase excitement. Defense simulations, on the other hand, overwhelmingly stress realistic environments and engagement situations. The interactions are *serious* in nature" (NRC 1997, 27, emphasis added). Published five years after this report, as *the* watershed game in the serious games movement *America's Army* arguably changed this stark distinction between the fun and the serious, and demonstrated that a piece of military software can be both.

These significant "cultural barriers" and differences between the defense simulation industry and the commercial video game industry have become less apparent in certain contexts as relationships become institutionalized through entities such as the ICT, which was a direct result of the publication of the *Modeling and Simulation* report. The discourse of "cultural barriers" was present throughout the history of *America's Army* as an indigenous explanation that both military personnel and developers provided about the causes of work conflicts between Army Game Project institutions. Such explanations point to larger issues outlined in previous chapters in regards to military efforts in drafting the cognitariat into its domain. While it is arguably an overly simplistic understanding, it highlights how separate elements of the theoretical "military entertainment complex" perceive themselves in relation to one another—not as a unified whole, but as a cosmos of separate cultural spheres.

The Evolution of a Military Game

The Committee on Modeling and Simulation of the National Research Council, which published *Modeling and Simulation* (1997), was chaired by Mike Zyda, who is generally given credit for the composition of the report. Having made recommendations in the report for a framework sponsoring collaborations and connections between the entertainment and defense industries through an academic context, Zyda (then a professor at the Naval Postgraduate School (NPS) in Monterey, California) subsequently drafted a proposal for the creation of the Institute for Creative Technologies (ICT) to address these recommendations. This proposal was funded in 1999 by an initial $45 million grant and renewed in 2004 at $100 million, at the time the largest research grant ever received by the University of Southern California (USC). A well-funded and well-established institute, the ICT went on to produce such games as *Full Spectrum Warrior*, which in its original noncommercial iteration was a military officer simulation trainer. Zyda, however, was not hired as the director of the ICT once it became funded and, disgruntled by what he perceived as a betrayal, started his own research institution in 2000 at the NPS, called the MOVES (Modeling, Virtual Environments, and Simulation) Institute.[4]

These events occurred at about the same time as Wardynski's fabled "epiphany" in army recruitment practices, and he was actively searching for viable locations for the development of a video game project. Following discussions Wardynski and Zyda agreed that the Army Game Project would be suitable for MOVES and the NPS, a research institution with primarily military officers pursuing master's and doctoral degrees. "MOVES was just the sort of environment that Casey [Wardynski] needed," a published *America's Army* manuscript claims (Davis and Bossant 2004, 20). Officially beginning in May 2000, the project was coded "Operation Star Fighter" after *The Last Starfighter* (1984), a film in which a boy, after scoring a perfect score on an arcade space game, is recruited by aliens to save the universe by piloting a real version of the game's ship in a space war.[5] The expertise of NPS researchers such as professor Mike Capps (the original executive producer of *America's Army*, who later became the president of game industry giant Epic Games) was "piped into the game," and members of the development team visited nineteen army posts for the purposes of gathering reference material for implementation into the game (Davis and Bossant 2004, 10–11). Epic Games' Unreal Engine 2 was licensed as crucial commercial middleware for the game's design (see chapter 3). This move was critical to the game's initial success, as versions of Unreal Engine form the basis for a great number of popular games and it is a development tool with which both hard-core gamers and game developers are generally familiar.

When the project was progressing more slowly than anticipated, Zyda hired a cadre of game industry veterans who knew one another from their work at Electronic Arts (EA)—Alex Mayberry ([Dev]Abraxas, *America's Army* creative director), Jesse McCree ([Dev]rayGunn, *America's Army* lead designer), and Phillip Bossant ([Dev]whatever, *America's Army* art director)—to take on the role of team leaders for the project. (Mayberry and McCree later joined Blizzard Entertainment to become the lead game producer and lead level designer of the much-acclaimed *World of Warcraft*.) This cadre of leaders built a talented development team that consisted at its largest of twenty-eight mostly young and relatively inexperienced, but dedicated, civilian game developers. Their dual requirements were difficult but not insurmountable: They had to put together not merely a fun and compelling game, but one that advertised the U.S. Army in a way that would market potential army careers to players.

One individual was hired straight out of high school for his depth of knowledge in military weapons and game design. An *America's Army* developer recalled this early development period at MOVES, explaining to me that when he first came to the project "there was no real precedent. Some of the people had [game] industry experience, but for most it was their first gig. And they threw together an amazing piece of software for 1.0, coming from where they were [and] trying to meet the requirements." He echoed a sentiment that I heard repeated often to describe almost every period in the development history of *America's Army*, saying that the work process was like "flying by the seat of your pants." Phillip Bossant also described this early period of the project as being "an intense time from December 2001 to July 2002. We basically rebuilt the game and started over. That's not an ideal amount of time and there weren't that many of us. It was a risky adventure; none of us knew if we could succeed or not."

Despite these doubts, the game debuted in June 2002 at the Electronic Entertainment Expo (E3) to much pageantry and spectacle. It was released to the general public for PC gaming one month later, on July 4, as the very first game to use the much-anticipated Unreal Engine 2, which, among a whole slate of other improvements, featured improved graphical and rendering capabilities. *America's Army: Recon* was the official title of version 1.0, and though it was met with initial skepticism by players, it proved many wrong. Michael "Ace" Abuchon ([Dev]Ace-Killa), an early fan and volunteer beta tester of the game who later became its lead designer, did not expect anything, "because the army is good at making games—yeah, right! But it was the Unreal Engine 2, so it was interesting." On the morning of its release, July 4, 2002, he went to buy the game *Warcraft 3*, which had been released the previous day, but before he installed that game he downloaded *America's Army: Recon 1.0*. "And, funny enough, it was a week before I opened up *Warcraft 3*."

The relatively small project that had begun under the auspices of a navy research institute and a West Point economic analysis center suddenly became headlines in the gaming industry. "With the success of *America's Army*," Ed Halter writes, "the real America's Army had, for a moment, become video-game industry rock stars, at a time when that industry itself had taken a quantum leap into the mainstream consciousness and entertainment business credibility" (2006, xvii). The sudden popularity took the development team by surprise. With the initial difficulties of putting together the *America's Army: Recon 1.0* release, they were happy to have survived. But what they were not prepared for were the kinds of "cultural barriers" in business practices that were described in Zyda's *Modelling and Simulation* report and that they felt were becoming more apparent. As Phillip Bossant put it, they still were unable to fully and "expertly live in two worlds at the same time—one foot in the entertainment industry, one foot in the government."

For the next several years, *America's Army* and the military came to define and dominate the emergent "serious games" industry, then the new buzzword in interactive entertainment, and the military contracting sector effectively colonized much of the press and industry attention at expos such as E3, the Game Developers Conference, and the Serious Games Summit. This military takeover of the games industry was unambiguously portrayed at E3 2003, one year after the game's release, as actual army soldiers rappelled from helicopters hovering over the Los Angeles Convention Center and stormed through conference attendees into the building to "secure" it (Halter 2006, vii–viii). Indeed, a more generally militarized framework became more apparent throughout the United States at this time, particularly in the national broadcasting networks, as the invasion and occupation of Iraq unfolded through the news media in a spectacularly cinematic fashion (Stahl 2007). In 2003 a study discovered that players of *America's Army* used the game as a means to more closely draw an experiential connection to the invasion of Iraq, sometimes simultaneously playing the game while listening to news reports. Fan communities and clans of players, such as Christian groups, were appropriating the game in a variety of ways, adding through proselytization, protest, and a variety of special interest communities what game scholars call "emergent" behavior to the intended functions and original design of the game (Li 2003).

The development studio at MOVES continued releasing updates to the game on a semi-regular schedule. After Mike Capps left the team as executive producer following the release of version 1.0, Alex Mayberry was promoted to the position as executive producer/creative director of the team. Though they met quarterly with Wardynski and planned out each release at these meetings, no overarching long-term vision regarding the game's development cycle was in place. Wardynski would provide feedback, give the stamp of approval, and provide general goals for the next release. "He would say things like, 'We really want to get an anti-vehicular weapon, the AT4 [in the game]. They're about to launch the XM25, so we want to get that in.' And we would say, 'that's going to cost this much,' and we would end up with some list of features for the next release."

The developers, however, came to realize that they needed a greater organizational structure with project scheduling. Army project managers from OEMA started giving the development team "feature creep" by insisting on extra features for upcoming releases without scheduling the features into the development workload or costs. Developers were subjected to army requirements that became moving targets, and it seemed to them that direction by Wardynski became increasingly "erratic." This contributed to a generally antagonistic feeling in the office toward the army. Despite the organizational support provided by Zyda's MOVES and the rock star status that the game had achieved following its initial release, the project was hopelessly underfunded and risked falling apart.

By October 2003, when they shipped *America's Army: Special Forces* (version 2.0), the team was suffering from "army burnout" and "the army was definitely the bad guy at that time." One anonymous game developer wrote in a forum that around this time the game had hit the third-ranking spot for total number of online players worldwide, and OEMA

> started complaining about how we weren't meeting their expectations. We began to read news stories interviewing Army personnel who talked about how they had built the game. The Navy started to get pissed at the Army because there was never any mention that the game was actually built within a Naval think-tank. A lot of political fights over the project broke out not only between the Army and the Navy, but within different divisions of the Army itself. When the project was just a fly-by-night rogue mission, no one paid much attention to it. Once the Army figured out that the game was the single most successful marketing campaign they'd ever launched (at one-third of 1% of their annual advertising budget), we suddenly came under a very big microscope.[6]

The sentiment of disillusion was further enhanced by the game's cadre of leaders, including executive producer Alex Mayberry, who by that time had "already moved on mentally." Mayberry, art director Phillip Bossant, and lead designer Jesse McCree had approached the project as entrepreneurs and saw it as a transitional position for collecting a talented team to work on other non-army commercial game development projects. Following the success of the initial release they began looking for ways to move the team into a new independent game development company to be named Arsenal Interactive. In the fall of 2003 the team had a "hell of a pipeline" and everybody knew their responsibilities. "The vibe [of the studio] was moving toward wanting to move away from NPS and become more commercialized. Alex and Jesse were planting the seeds in the team, and you could see it taking place." The studio began holding meetings about the entire team leaving to a new California location in either Bakersfield or San Francisco. Mayberry and McCree began searching their game industry connections for startup funding "to set up a new company and basically walk out on the army."

Rumors began circulating throughout the office that the army itself was looking for a new development team to replace the one at MOVES, and this additionally motivated the team to search actively for opportunities to partner with game publishers, especially Electronic Arts (EA) and Activision. Unbeknownst to either OEMA or MOVES, *America's Army* artists were assigned projects to do work for both EA and Activision, "on Army computers and on Army time," with one artist reportedly spending about three months of full-time work on a *Wolfenstein* game character prototype for publisher Activision. Another developer was reportedly doing level design for EA. "We had like three bids, and they all wanted us to do work for them to prove [our worth]. We had guys doing all kinds of work. [Someone else] was doing totally different work for a totally different game. We had a logo. We made a movie for Arsenal Interactive."

The budding mutiny reached levels of absurdity that winter, when Wardynski was scheduled to visit the development studio for a quarterly *America's Army* progress report. A developer had mistakenly scheduled a visit with Activision to discuss possibilities about startup funding for Arsenal Interactive at the exact time of Wardynski's visit. While some developers were at the Hilton in Monterey, California, fielding Activision, Wardynski was with others at the Hyatt next door. "The Army never knew, and the colonel left."

Soon enough, however, the army did catch wind of the extracurricular activities of the development team. On March 8, 2004, when the developers showed up to work, they discovered Wardynski there in the conference room, in full dress uniform—and "he never wears full dress uniform." Accompanying Wardynski was his commanding officer, the Deputy Assistant Secretary of the Army, John McLaurin, along with several other army officers. Mayberry and McCree were fired on the spot, and "of course the team just blows up, and gets all rowdy, and people started saying, 'well I'm out too.'" Several developers voluntarily left, but most were convinced to stay on the project by Philip Bossant, who took over as the interim executive producer/art director. Bossant himself was planning on walking out as well, but Mayberry and McCree convinced him to stay in order to keep the team together, still with the dream of eventually setting up Arsenal Interactive by way of an intact team of *America's Army* developers.

Although the legal ramifications of fraud were potentially severe, and "the colonel was really pissed off," the army decided that it was in their best interest not to pursue additional punishment to the development team besides the top-level firings. A higher-level political battle centering on *America's Army* and involving the navy, army, and air force had been simmering since the previous summer. The fallout from this interservice rivalry resulted in the army announcing, at the same meeting, that they were moving development of the game away from the Naval Postgraduate School and MOVES, and setting up a new army-managed office at the nearby decommissioned base at Fort Ord.

Between January and April 2004, when *America's Army* was being exhibited at the San Francisco Yerba Buena Center for the Arts' exhibit, "Bang the Machine: Computer Gaming Art and Artifacts" (Chapman 2004), a multilevel conflict between Wardynski's OEMA and Zyda's umbrella institution, the Naval Postgraduate School (NPS), had come to a head. At the conflict's center was the issue of publishing credit and publicity from the game, which the NPS wished to share with the army. Wardynski and OEMA, however, did not want the navy to gain any press from its central role in developing an army game, as this would undermine marketing claims then being made about the product's authenticity as a game "designed, developed, and published by the U.S. Army."

Earlier, in July 2003, the superintendent of the NPS had told OEMA that if the navy school could not obtain any publicity from their involvement in the Army Game Project, then Wardynski would have to find another host. In the meantime, however, Wardynski encouraged Zyda to seek out other sources of income for the NPS by building new military training tools that used material from *America's Army* as spin-off technology to sell to other U.S. government entities. Wardynski pointed Zyda to the air force as a potential customer, and Zyda's MOVES Institute at the NPS created a convoy protection scenario, using *America's Army* software, for the air force to use as a soldier trainer. This move, however, was deemed by auditors as an "augmentation of federal appropriations" from outside sources, without federal approval. Money allocated by the Department of Defense to the Army's *America's Army* project was illegally used on the air force project by MOVES. Zyda reportedly did not realize the legal parameters of "augmentation" prior to taking on the air force project, and felt set up by Wardynski.

Wardynski later filed a formal complaint regarding this partnership to the Department of Defense Office of Inspector General to investigate mismanagement of the Army Game Project by the MOVES. In a report published in 2005 the office found that the MOVES had "made 45 improper charges totaling nearly $500,000 to the Army Game Project and an Air Force Project," "lacked the capability to perform a major portion of work on the project," and had implemented management practices that had the "appearance of nepotism" (2005, i–ii). These factors, in addition to what appears to have been a developing personal conflict between Wardynski and Zyda, provided OEMA with a reason to remove its association with the MOVES and take complete control of (and credit for) the Army Game Project. When I interviewed him in the summer of 2006 Mike Zyda was still discernibly bitter about the whole situation, interspersing every sentence with a least a few obscenities when talking about that period. Zyda speculates that the air force project debacle was manufactured by Wardynski after the NPS made it clear that the army would have to share credit for the development of *America's Army* with the navy.

With the project now under its complete control, Wardynski's OEMA began bringing in other entities and expanding the Army Game Project beyond its original parameters as an online PC game. The Fort Ord studio was renamed the *America's Army* Public Applications (AAPA), and began to share the game's "assets"—units of game art, characters, weapons, textures, particle effects, animations, and designs—with other new Army Game Project organizations. The air force project had shown that assets were cheaply reusable for other government and defense projects, compared to typical costs of ordering training software for operating weapons systems from large defense contractors. A private studio in Raleigh, North Carolina, began work on these types of military trainers, reusing *America's Army* assets. SimWars Inc., later renamed Virtual Heroes, was a subcontractor for what was known as *America's Army* Government Applications (AAGA). Yet another team at Picatinny Arsenal in New Jersey, called *America's Army* Future Applications (AAFA), began work on simulation trainers and weapons prototyping. "We had these three different organizations that were ostensibly to produce assets for each other," one developer told me, "but they were producing at a different level of quality. The Picatinny guys were not artists."

With the successful implementation of the Javelin Basic Skills Trainer, a cost-saving training system that simulated the expensive Javelin missile system (costing $86,000 per missile), a slate of other training simulators began development at these institutions, including one made for the U.S. Secret Service. One training simulation was developed in 2005 in cooperation with the Sandia National Laboratories and the J.F.K. Special Warfare Center to train soldiers in cross-cultural communication with local civilians and "cultural awareness."[7] Other products implemented by the Army Game Project were intended to save money by reducing boot camp dropout rates (and added army costs) for soldiers by mentally preparing new recruits for rudimentary aspects of basic training and military life.[8]

The Army Game Project also executed a commercial partnership with video game publisher Ubisoft shortly after the move to Fort Ord. Under this agreement Ubisoft licensed the *America's Army* title to build two totally separate games. The first, for the Xbox and PlayStation 2, was *America's Army: Rise of a Soldier*, developed by the private studio Secret Level and published for commercial release by Ubisoft in 2005. The game met with mixed reviews but was enough of a success to merit a sequel for the Xbox 360, *America's Army: True Soldiers*, which was rushed through development and published by Ubisoft in 2007. *True Soldiers* received abysmal reviews, providing ample reason for Wardynski to cancel the partnership with Ubisoft following its release. Game developer Zombie Studios,[9] data analytics and software distribution company Pragmatic Solutions, marketing firm Ignited (see fig. 15), and contracting organization Digital Consulting Services each joined the Army Game Project at varying points, and each company benefited significantly from the business opportunities made available by their membership.

However, the core AAPA development team, newly relocated to Fort

Ord, was taking a long time to recover from its self-imposed crisis, and developers were leaving on a regular basis following the firings of Mayberry and McCree. The employment turnover during this time was so high that by 2007 only six of the twenty-eight team members from early 2004 were still working at the studio; when *America's Army 3* was released in 2009 only two of this original group remained. Due to the uncertainty of maintaining a viable core development team, OEMA became worried that the entire AAPA team would disintegrate, and began taking measures against this happening. One day in the summer of 2004 several individuals from the AAGA offices in North Carolina arrived without warning at the AAPA studio on Wardynski's authority, "with hard drives, USB keys. They just charge into the office to 'extract the data.' They didn't say, 'hey, we're your replacements if you guys fuck up, and we're taking everything you have because we're not sure you're going to be around next week,'" but that was the underlying message that was sent to the AAPA team.

Following the suppressed mutiny of Mayberry and McCree, this was the first of many efforts on Wardynski's part to control the game development team, either by manufacturing competition, imposing an outsider authority figure onto the development process, simply firing those who were deemed most problematic, or combining two or more of these approaches. A studio orientation of paranoia toward nonstudio "outsiders" associated with the Army Game Project began with this incident, and continued throughout my own fieldwork at the studio. I, too, was subject to suspicion when I first arrived at the California office for two weeks in 2007 when a developer, as the mouthpiece of the whole team, questioned me for two hours about my research project in order to discern whether I was a "spy" sent by Wardynski or another Army Game Project team to monitor them.

The initial "data extraction" interaction with the new AAGA team from North Carolina colored the relationship between the two teams. The California AAPA team was envious of the AAGA team's status within an independent company (Virtual Heroes), which was something that Mayberry and McCree had hoped to achieve. They also suspected that executives at Virtual Heroes wanted more, in addition to the AAGA contract for simulation trainers. When Wardynski announced that Philip DeLuca

([Dev]Skippy) would become the new executive producer of the AAPA team, it looked exactly as if the executives at Virtual Heroes were sending their own choice of leadership to California. "Come to find out, [DeLuca] was [their] buddy, and we already hated [them]."

"When I was first approached by [the executives at Virtual Heroes, they were] saying that [they were] going to be given the directorship of the entire *America's Army* program, which would be Pub Apps [AAPA], Gov Apps [AAGA], and Future Apps [AAFA]," DeLuca explained to me.

The actual environment was incredibly toxic when I got there [. . .] so I fired [the lead programmer] the day I got there. I also let some other people go because they were complicit in what amounts to fraud. I figured the team had defrauded the government by a minimum of $200,000 because they claimed to be working on something, never delivered that something, and instead used all of their time to [. . .] pitch to set up their own company. And I understand why they did it—they were dissatisfied with the government and how the army was managing them. [The army] didn't understand that video game development is comprised of a series of negotiations. They are used to giving an order and essentially having the person carry it out. So they weren't prepared for that back and forth.

DeLuca's actions and management style further demoralized the now-small team that was "already running out of steam." This factor, combined with DeLuca's posting of an antagonistic game forum message directed at *America's Army* hackers, which acknowledged (against Wardynski's wishes) that the army could indeed track individuals based on their IP address,[10] led to DeLuca's six-month contract not being renewed in April 2005. Philip Bossant once again stepped in, this time as the permanent executive producer.

DeLuca told me that, at that time, executives at Virtual Heroes were "competing for all intents and purposes for control of the project, [making the case that] because of [their] central role in [AAGA . . . they] should actually take [AAPA] and run it." It was becoming apparent that a more centralized restructuring of the entire project was necessary in order to bring all of the disparate elements to work together in a more organized, and less antagonistic, fashion. Virtual Heroes began courting the disaffected AAPA employees remaining on the diminished California team to move to North Carolina. These efforts were to also be Mike Zyda's revenge for losing the project from MOVES, since Zyda sat on the corporate advisory board for Virtual Heroes, unbeknownst to Wardynski. The attempts by executives at Virtual Heroes to control the AAPA ultimately proved ineffective, stymied in part by what appears to have been a personal rivalry with an army major working at OEMA under Wardynski.

As had happened previously, the project in the midst of its growth was plagued by crisis, personal and institutional rivalries, and a lack of mutual understanding of the varying needs of game developers, government contractors, and military personnel. Reflecting on this, Phil DeLuca offered a retrospective analysis of the situation by the time of his departure in the spring of 2005:

> The colonel's idea was fundamentally brilliant. It demonstrated a level of insight as to what the army needed, and connected it to a social phenomenon that he was not familiar with, and he put it together, and it was absa-fucking-lutely brilliant. Now, the execution was poor, and that was definitely his fault. He selected these two majors, and one of them was really capable and driven and really intense, and another was . . . corrupt. And that's his fault! The colonel fucked up, and he really doesn't accept that he was flawed. He views the flaws as being in the civilians, who were ultimately responsible for implementing the application. [. . .] He should have turned it over to a game development company. And he should have had a board that he could go to and ask, "Should we be spending $3 million [a year] on a game and $10 million [a year] on its marketing campaign?"

With his retirement looming Wardynski realized that there was a need to ensure the long-term viability of the Army Game Project, and he knew that OEMA was not the answer. As a research institution at West Point, OEMA's mission was to make recommendations and prototypes, the implementation of which would be carried out by other entities; OEMA had never been meant to be the permanent home of the Army Game Project. With the goal of an eventual transition in mind, in 2005 OEMA began sharing project responsibilities with the Software Engineering Directorate (SED) at Redstone Arsenal, near Huntsville, Alabama. Redstone Arsenal hosts a number of rocket science research and development centers, including NASA's Marshal Space Flight Center and the U.S. Army's Aviation and Missile Command. Well-known space programs (Gemini, Saturn, Mercury) and army weapons systems (e.g., Patriot and Javelin missiles; Apache, Chinook, and Black Hawk helicopters) are some of the many programs originating from Redstone Arsenal. Compared with these extensive programs at Redstone Arsenal the SED was a small institution, and, like the other companies involved in the project, it made *America's Army* its poster child.

The development of the many soldier trainers based on the *America's Army* platform transitioned to the SED in 2005, while Virtual Heroes and other companies continued to contribute to various projects. At the highest level, the SED project managers of these gaming and simulation training programs were employees of the U.S. government, while other individuals working at the SED were employees of a hodgepodge of large military contracting companies such as Northrop Grumman, Lockheed Martin, and SAIC (Science Applications International Corporation, now known as Leidos).

Michael Bode ([Dev]Bode) worked as an employee of Northrop Grumman at the SED as a project manager for various *America's Army* Basic Skills Trainers. He specified how in this labor context the hierarchy of contracting was "an important cultural thing." Management of projects almost always falls into the hands of U.S. government civilian employees, underneath whom are additional hierarchies. "Prime" contractors are those individuals working for companies that hold the primary government contract for a project. At the lower levels of the hierarchy of government contracting are those employees known as "team members," who work for companies that are subcontracted by the prime contractor. "If you are not government, the government people will treat you differently. It's like being in a club. It's partly because they are trained like that, and educated that they can communicate certain things to contractors, and can't do certain things."[11]

As one of the largest U.S. Department of Defense contractors, SAIC (now Leidos) was the "prime" contractor for the Army Game Project, enabling money to pass from the government to "team member" companies, and then down the line to the employees of those companies. At each stage the overhead for managing the game's development was multiplied by each contracting institution. One illustrative example that was recounted to me by an *America's Army* executive concerned the salaries of game developers at the AAPA, who were directly employed by a "team member" company called Digital Consulting Services (DCS). An AAPA game developer being paid, for example, $50,000 by DCS would allow DCS to bill the "prime" contractor SAIC around $100,000. SAIC would, in turn, bill the U.S. government around $150,000 for fees directly related to the management of this one employee. Though SAIC, ranked at number 245 in the Fortune 500 list with $10.6 billion in annual revenue in 2013,[12] was the holder of the prime contract for *America's Army* with the U.S. government, it had very little presence in the day-to-day activities of most parts of the Army Game Project and zero presence at the AAPA game studio. Many *America's Army* developers had never heard of SAIC.

This government contracting arrangement was a recurring problem from the point of view of the California development studio, which "always felt like we're being held at a distance." While AAPA game developers and their employer, Digital Consulting Services, were "team members" who were quite arguably producing the core product of the Army Game Project—the PC game *America's Army*—they were very much on the outskirts of the contracting hierarchy. "They are not SAIC, so they are not prime, and so they are kind of looked down upon by SAIC employees. They're not government, so [they are] on the low end of the totem pole in that regard."

When the SED first came on board the project, AAPA developers hoped that some of the management problems that had plagued the team, such as the persistent issue of "feature creep" requests by OEMA infringing on previously agreed-on workload timelines, would be mitigated. Erich Iveans ([Dev]Pye) recalled how during their first interaction with SED the AAPA team detailed lists of such issues to the SED director, Frank Blackwell, "just demand after demand that we couldn't meet and still produce the game." Blackwell, he recounted,

was sitting at the conference table and saying, "I find this hard to believe, that's just not possible." The second half of the day, [an army officer from OEMA] shows up and he goes, "The AUSA [Association of the U.S. Army] meetings are coming up, and I've promised everyone that you are going to make a video about Sergeant Smith," this guy who was posthumously awarded a Congressional Medal of Honor for his combat actions. "Not only are you going to make this video of that action in the game, we're going to do it at this resolution for projecting it on three wide screens. It's due in two months—let's go!" We could not have asked for a better example of how messed up things were. At the end of that day, Frank Blackwell said to us, "I need to go to Colonel Wardynski and talk to him, because I've figured out the problem, and the problem is him."

The developers continued releasing new updates for the game on a regular basis and were "successful at pulling off those miracle moments to keep us going," such as producing the aforementioned project about Sergeant Smith while also working on the game they were hired to make. Despite their petitioning SED with their woes, however, they were never successful at setting reasonable expectations for their managers. In a move that quite possibly saved the studio from complete implosion, the AAPA changed locations once again in 2006 to Emeryville, a small city sandwiched between Berkeley, Oakland, and San Francisco Bay. Most of the small development team was happy to make the move north to a more urban and cosmopolitan center, and the move deliberately sought to take advantage of closer contacts with the electronic entertainment industry by bringing the office into the cultural fold of Silicon Valley and the Bay Area. A variety of digital entertainment companies such as Pixar and Electronic Arts' Maxis studio (developers of *The Sims*, *Spore*, and *SimCity*) were in close proximity to the AAPA. Developers liked to remark that they shared a Starbucks with video game industry celebrity Will Wright, who would regularly be seen during coffee breaks and who once came to visit the studio.

The Emeryville studio was where I found my fieldwork home within the Army Game Project, first arriving there in September 2006 and visiting regularly—often for months at a time—until June 2009. In autumn 2006 they had just put out a major release, *America's Army: Overwatch* (version 2.7), a high point in the franchise's history that was neverthe-less described as being "a goddamn miracle." By that point the studio had reestablished a systematic workflow pipeline that made for efficient development. New graduates from the nearby Ex'pression College for Digital Arts made an easy transition to work at the studio, the location of which was deliberately chosen due to its close proximity to the school, and an intern program was set up between the two organizations.

The team was finally able to create a space that felt like a typically casual and relaxed game development studio, and this contributed to a greater sense of normalcy as they transitioned to the production of *America's Army 3* in 2007. Other Army Game Project initiatives materi-alized in 2007 as well, including the Virtual Army Experience, a major project that the SED, Ignited, Zombie, and the AAPA produced collabo-ratively (see chapter 4). Additional commercial industry partnerships like an *America's Army* arcade game and a cell phone game, both pub-lished in 2007, resulted in products that made the franchise's claims to authenticity and realism absurd (see fig. 16).[13] Ubisoft's *America's Army: True Soldiers* flop was also released in 2007. When they worked out as anticipated, such commercial arrangements were win-win situations for both institutions, providing free advertising opportunities to the army while giving the licensing organization the ability to create an "official" army game to sell for profit. Control over content, though, had always been an important issue that Wardynski had been loath to relinquish. The dubious quality of these games in terms of both playability and their desired representation of the army led to a more cautious approach in terms of future game industry relationships.

Noncommercial industry partnerships for use of the *America's Army* platform involved a very successful project now used by the Walter Reed Army Medical Center involving a driving simulation for wounded sol-diers using prosthetics or needing assistance in reacclimating to the civilian world.[14] A soldier could now potentially go through recruitment, training, and post-trauma therapy using the *America's Army* platform, thus meshing the life cycle of the game software with that of the soldier (Allen 2015). Collaboration with the nonprofit organization Project Lead the Way, also starting in 2008, gave the organization use of the platform for teaching middle and high school students physics through virtual simulation experiments.[15] Later, NASA's "first-person explorer" serious game *Moonbase Alpha* (2010) was developed in partnership with Virtual Heroes, NASA Learning Technologies, and the SED using the *America's Army* platform. The free game—winner of the 2010 Serious Games Showcase and Challenge "Government" category—simulates moon life in a near-future scenario, and like *America's Army* it encourages teamwork between its players in a digital institutional setting.

New updates to *America's Army: Special Forces*, released in November 2003 (version 2.0), were being developed and released until April 2009 (version 2.8.5). This six-year release cycle for a single game is astonishing, and highly unusual in an industry full of games that have a lifespan of several months to a few years at most. During these years military first-person shooters (FPS), a genre of games that the original *America's Army* helped define and build, became demonstrably popular through successful game franchises like *Call of Duty, Medal of Honor, Conflict, SOCOM,* and *Battlefield. America's Army* maintained a core group of dedicated players who communicated regularly with developers like producer Erich Iveans ([Dev]Pye) in official online forums, but the pull of a free game became less pronounced over the years as the game's graphic technology and slower style of gameplay was unable to keep pace with the industry. The rate of registered users of the game dropped considerably as newer, flashier products came to market.

While *America's Army* was ostensibly a game targeting a younger population to encourage the consideration of the army as a viable career choice, a discernibly older group of gamers played the game. It was, in the words of the developers, a "thinking man's tactical shooter" that did not require as much "twitch skill" as newer, more individualistically competitive FPS games. The play style deliberately encouraged in *America's Army* also influenced who continued playing since "one of the core goals [of *America's Army* is] that a well-coordinated team should always be able to beat a more individually talented, random group of people."

Part of the reason for the six-year longevity in the development of *America's Army: Special Forces*, despite the gradual obsolescence of the game for younger players, was that the building of *America's Army 3* did not progress very smoothly. Developers recounted to me how there was a lack of leadership and vision at the California studio in terms of what the finished product should be, and how the lead designer who had worked on the team for many years contributed to the standstill by refusing to delegate responsibility. Wardynski and the SED waited impatiently through 2007 and early 2008 for progress toward a finished product that never materialized, and both OEMA and the SED began having discussions regarding the effectiveness of maintaining a team in California in the first place. Eventually Mike Bode was sent from Alabama to California in the spring of 2008 to become the co-executive producer with Phillip Bossant. "In [Wardynski's] eyes Phillip had failed," a developer confided, "and I can't completely disagree with that." Yet at the same time for the developers "it felt like there was shit going on up in the lofty perches of the army side that was buffeting us around in ways that we didn't necessarily fully understand or even get exposed to."

There gradually became implemented a more hierarchical chain of command, placing the SED as the mediator between OEMA and the developers, that prevented significant communication between the game producers in California and OEMA. This contrast with the earlier years of development was due to the centralizing force of the SED, which came to direct more of the requirements in the development of the game. Developers speculated that after Wardynski's expected retirement in 2010 the SED would become the permanent home for *America's Army*, and this indeed was the ultimate goal of the Directorate's leaders. With the idea of decapitating the leadership of the California team in order to implement a smoother transition of the game's development to the SED post-release, Mike Bode "came with instructions to clean house on management. He didn't do it because he realized how important some people were to the project."

Wardynski, however, wanted a "price for failure" in the delay of *America's Army 3*. Unbeknownst to most of the developers, the delay in production by late 2008 had solidified Wardynski's resolve to shut down the studio after the release of the game and move the game's production entirely to the SED, despite Bode's protests that the SED, as a government software development institution, lacked the video game industry talent pool capable of taking on the project effectively. But having previously experienced near-implosions of the project due to its leadership, Wardynski was hardened in implementing a preemptive-strike approach to dealing with the California development team. Recounting the plot of a movie that told the story of a Civil War unit whose mutiny was forestalled by the execution of its leaders, Wardynski stepped in and directed Bode to fire Bossant, a studio favorite, along with another long-time and critically knowledgeable producer in the summer of 2008. An additional experienced designer and team leader from the MOVES era quit following this, reportedly explaining his decision to leave to the entire team by saying simply, "Shit is unfun."

When I began open-ended interviews with *America's Army* game developers soon after this event, a large portion of what developers wanted to talk about involved what they termed as being "a huge clusterfuck of project management" that was only intensified by the firings. One level designer discussed how "It doesn't even matter when we say no" to "unrealistic demands. It is crazy land." Although this level designer enjoyed the challenge, it felt

> like we are really being thrown into the deep end. [. . .] You have these crazy requirements that are difficult to meet coming at you from people who are intractable and on whom you have no leverage. You got moving targets, and that's all just part of the job. Working in constraints fundamentally makes you do better work, so I'm into that. [But] the wriggle room you have is so small and the creativity you have got to bring to the problem is so considerable. And you have to solve all the problems at once: What is going to meet the requirements of the army; actually reflect legitimately useful information about the [Military Occupational Specialties of soldiers]; use real equipment; be something that we can create the art for in the time we have; [and], on top of that, have a roadmap for all of this stuff to roll out over the next five years so that any given thing we are making doesn't just fuck everything that came before it with some fundamental change. And to do that with only six dudes on staff who can program, [who already have] no time.

When I later visited the SED at Redstone Arsenal I realized that workers there experienced parallel pressures but very different conditions, which were not conducive to managing a video game being developed over two thousand miles away by game developers of a very different cultural mentality than their government managers in Alabama. No electronic devices from off-base were allowed in the buildings—no cell phones, USB devices, cameras, iPods, voice recorders, and definitely no laptops.[16] Such security conditions were a strain for everyone involved, especially the project managers, one of whom described her work to me as being in a state that is "always in panic mode" due to the multiple pressures and demands. During a visit with another SED project manager, he told me that he had received forty-eight emails over the course of my single hour visiting his office. These workplace factors could perhaps partially explain a series of SED purchasing mishaps in 2008, in which software licenses for the use of critical middleware necessary for the California team were not obtained.[17] These lapses—which the California team believed reflected either SED incompetence, deliberate sabotage, or both—caused game development to come to a near standstill at several points and created further tension when the blame for such delays was placed squarely on the California team by the SED.

The relationship between the game developers and their management at SED and OEMA was sometimes explained in indigenous terms by the developers, who would say that these conflicts, at the core, arose from cultural differences. "Every time we try to bring in common sense the government fucks it up with their weird justifications or rules that don't make any sense to our culture," one developer told me in frustration. Another former developer reflected on his experiences in a similar way, writing that "there was a magic couple of years there where two totally alien cultures came together to do something cool."[18] Though it is most likely too simplistic an explanation, the language of cultural difference highlights how *America's Army* is far more than the sum of what the army says it is—a video game "designed, developed, and deployed by the U.S. Army." As an example *par excellence* of the "military entertainment complex," the history of *America's Army* reveals a contingent history of relationships that is indeed very complex.

The relationships I have described here highlight anthropologist David Graeber's observation that "totalities are always creatures of the imagination. Nations, societies, ideologies, closed systems . . . none of these really exist. Reality is always infinitely messier than that—even if the belief that they exist is an undeniable social force" (2004, 13). The power of the concept of the "complex" (e.g., "military industrial complex") is in its ability to obfuscate multifaceted processes by making it appear as if the reality of convoluted negotiations, rivalries, and collaborations is actually smooth, logical, and homogeneous. The idea of "the network," I would argue, achieves a similar result of affording more power to a phenomenon than it deserves.

I went to the Army Game Project in search of a network of interoperable and exchangeable entities, people, and organizations—but this proved largely elusive. What I found instead was a hierarchical assortment of military, government, commercial, and contracting institutions, factional and personal rivalries, a long history of disgruntled workers, and a mode of explaining away misunderstandings and conflicts through a generalizing language of cultural differences. Although institutions in the Army Game Project did ultimately have to cooperate with one another to a certain extent, there was an intense amount of competition between organizations over product content, funding, and reputation. Underlying all of this competition was a fundamentally business-driven motive of organizational self-preservation, especially for those businesses and entities that relied heavily or exclusively on Army Game Project funding in order to operate. Although a horizontal, deterritorialized, and virtual network of production did exist to a certain extent, as an army-sponsored project the Army Game Project was essentially a hierarchically and bureaucratically organized endeavor, "a feudal society existing within a democratic one," as several developers liked to say.

On the ground and inside its institutions, the picture of the Army Game Project was much more nuanced and factional than the seamless and idealized networked production model described by network and netwar theorists. Echoing Catherine Lutz's opening epigraph to this chapter, its history shows much more contingency than writers adhering to the canonical history of war games ever show. Institutions that produce military power, Lutz writes, are diverse, complex, and often incompetent. "Despite the perception that the military is unified and coherent, its projects are and long have been often as plural, political, and contested as the projects of other arms of the state" (2006, 603).

While OEMA claimed that *America's Army* was successful in helping the army recruit and hold on to the labor of talented soldiers, the accounts of *America's Army* that I uncovered through speaking to the game's developers point to a contrasting story of success and failure in the recruitment and retention of game development labor and in the management of the project itself.

6 The Labor of Virtual Soldiers

This is my opportunity for me to use you as a conduit to paint a picture of how it really goes down. If I get fired tomorrow, nobody's going to know, unless you write about it. [. . .] I think that you could at least be a conduit to tell everybody else what kinds of challenges we really face here.

America's Army developer, to the author, about his reasons for consenting to an interview

Recruiting the Developers

By the time the autumn of 2008 rolled around, I had situated myself full-time at the *America's Army* game development studios in Emeryville, California. Over the course of twenty months (2007–9), I had spent approximately seven months at this game studio, where *America's Army* 3 was under development in a nondescript office building overlooking San Francisco Bay, and I had come to know well many on the thirty-four-person development team. The workplace itself was a dark and comfortable maze of cubicles, meeting rooms, hallways, and offices. The characteristically quiet productivity of the work environment was punctuated by regular events such as morning meetings, conference calls, lunch and coffee breaks, play tests, guests visiting from other Army Game Project offices, and after-work ultimate Frisbee matches, gaming, and beers. I usually arrived in the morning and stayed until the late afternoon or evening, trying to stay as unobtrusive as possible in a demanding work environment, unless people were on break and in a talkative mood. Thanks to the generosity of the producers I had my own office situated among the quality assurance team, as well as a key to the studio that functioned during working hours and an *America's Army* email address, which helped me keep track of office communications, priorities, and outings.

One day after work, over beers with some of the developers, I had a laugh over my initial arrival there, when I was met by Phillip Bossant, at that time the game's executive producer. Bossant showed me around the office, and we gravitated toward the office kitchen, the intuitive choice for coffee and morning conversation. "Coffee is a big deal here. It fuels the team," he told me. We were met in the kitchen by a group of four uniformed men—some in full U.S. Army fatigues, others wearing digitized camo pants with regular T-shirts. Naturally I assumed that they were soldiers; it was the U.S. Army's video game studio, after all, and they were dressed in army gear. As conversation continued, I asked one of them how long he had been in the army, adding that I did not know that actual soldiers worked on the video game. He laughed and said, "Oh, we're civilians. We like to play at being in the army."

This statement stuck with me precisely because of its glibness and salience in achieving a blending between worlds that are typically talked about in contemporary American discourse as being oppositional and discrete from one another: the separate worlds of work and play, and those of the soldier and the civilian, both of which I discuss in detail in chapter 1. Of course the actual boundaries between these spheres (if they exist at all) are porous and eroding, and they have been becoming less visible for quite some time through multiple channels. In this book I have argued that the Army Game Project contributes to this blending, which enables the enlistment of civilian players as *virtual soldiers*—not only in the popular sense that they are soldiers playing in a virtual or simulated environment, but also in the sense that they are potential soldiers (in other words, virtually soldiers) who might fight in Iraq, Afghanistan, or elsewhere in the future. The term "virtual soldiers" can be used interchangeably, sometimes to connote one or both of these meanings simultaneously since they are not mutually exclusive. But the latter meaning of *virtual* is salient given the fact that versions of *America's Army* are also used in training enlisted soldiers for weapons familiarization and cultural awareness role-playing exercises.

Like the mythic and unreal enemies of their creation (see chapter 3), the developers of *America's Army* underwent a parallel imperative to flexibly adapt their labor to the mythic narratives of war. Through their work experiences the video game developers became a kind of hybrid soldier-civilian, possessors of expert military knowledge who worked within a liminal space between so-called military and nonmilitary spheres to translate this knowledge to video gamers and the larger public. Toward this end, their labor not only produced a finished software product, but also projected an affective, militarized ethos for marketing and public relations. This type of immaterial labor was mobilized to soften the stark distinctions between the categories of the gaming civilian and the working soldier. This amalgamation of categories, which is central to the creation and maintenance of virtual soldiering, engages in a playful but serious liminality, which is arguably an effective vehicle of militarization (see chapter 1); it is a post-Fordist magical construction that perpetuates war.

For the immaterial laborers working within the video game industry—with its precarious cycles of unemployment, eighty-hour weeks during "crunch time," and indistinguishable intermeshing between work and leisure time—the seemingly oxymoronic concepts of "playbor" (Dyer-Witheford and de Peuter 2009, 23–27) and "flexploitation" (Gray 2004), though not part of their everyday vocabulary, would accurately describe their everyday life. These post-Fordist realities characterized the industry in which the game developers of *America's Army* worked. They were, by and large, a group of individuals in pursuit of careers in game development or similar fields. As is often the case with soldiers who enlist in the U.S. military, it was principally economic and career advancement opportunities that led most *America's Army* game developers to choose work for a military contractor. Although a few of them had experiences with the military through past enlistment or employment, for most developers their work was the first extended period of contact that they had ever had with a military organization. It was a young group, with the vast majority of employees having less than five years of game development experience. Many were fresh graduates from Bay Area universities with degree programs in graphic arts, design, animation, and other software- and skills-related programs. Even by the standards of the demographically skewed video game industry employment norms, it was a beardy group of mostly twenty- to forty-year-old white male game developers.[1]

Most of the developers were avid video gamers. Some typically stayed at the game development studio hours after the end of the work day in order to use the studio computers and facilities for their personal enjoyment. One person told me, "All of these new games come out and you need to go check 'em out. For me, I feel like it's a part of my research and development. But if I didn't do this for a living, I would still [play games]." While sometimes they played as an individual activity, very often it was a collective, social enterprise of networked gaming that kept employees of *America's Army* playing together, either at the studio's computers or at their home computers.[2] Because such activities directly fed back into their development of the game, keeping them up to date about new games, news, technologies, and memes, these practices were encouraged by the game's producers, who sought to maintain the studio as a comfortable and stress-free space. During "crunch time," an unspecified period prior to the game's release when tasks were compressed into smaller windows of time, many would forgo their gaming and would stay late to work at the studio, sometimes sleeping there. In these experiences the game developers of *America's Army* differed little from the rest of the game development industry.

But the labor of *America's Army* game developers went beyond the mere development of the game, and entered into a resocializing, institutionalizing, and militarized process that crafted them into virtual soldiers. This emerged in part as a result of the subject material of their game, as level designers, animators, sound technicians, and artists necessarily had to be knowledgeable about the minute details of army uniforms, weapons, and doctrine. As I describe below, efforts undertaken to include the team under the institutional umbrella of the army further achieved this. Several developers also brought their past experiences and interests in the military to the development offices: two were veterans of the U.S. armed forces, while several others were gun enthusiasts, volunteer participants in live simulation training exercises for Bay Area police forces, and, of course, enthusiastic players of games that were often military-themed. One developer even left the team to run a successful business designing military gear and reviewing new weapons for sale on the civilian market.[3] With these influences the design team embodied a remarkable mix of militarized libertarian ideology, coupled with a hefty dose of Berkeley liberalism, hipster irony, and a sardonic disdain for almost anything to do with the Republican Party, especially Sarah Palin.

In this work environment the developers adopted to varying degrees the subjectivities of soldiers. This was particularly true in their thinking about their employment. The HBO mini-series *Generation Kill* (2008), based upon Evan Wright's book about his experiences as an embedded reporter with a marine unit during the 2003 invasion of Iraq (2004), was one of many shared narratives that shaped how several developers envisioned their work relations and relationships with outside institutions in terms of the military. Off-site managers at the SED in Alabama were compared to incompetent leaders in the film series, such as Captain America. Colonel Wardynski was the Godfather, another character in the series. And I, the anthropologist, was clearly in the position most analogous to the journalist Evan Wright: "I don't think of you as a spy anymore," a developer, Walker, told me after my first week in the office, "you're more like an embedded journalist, and that means we need to keep you alive." When I joined developers during countless in-studio playtests of their game, I came to understand that this sense of camaraderie also was brought about and sustained through the shared, and patently fun, experiences of virtual military combat in video games.

Later, in an interview, Walker expanded his analogy between the development team and army units, explaining to me that "this is an elite team. We are an elite squad of individuals. We have been chosen by the army to make this game. That's a big deal and I think a lot of team members take that for granted. [. . .] There are thirty people on-site here and four people off-site. That's a tight squad; that's a platoon-sized unit. That's exactly what that is, a platoon-sized element, and [the producer] runs around like the platoon sergeant. We got a design squad, an art squad, and [the executive producer] is like the lieutenant." For many army game developers, their exposure to some of the specialized experiences of soldiers became a meaningful way for them to include themselves within the greater institution of the army and identify with the situations of enlisted soldiers. Walker went as far as envisioning his work on the game, living in California away from many of his friends and family, in terms of an extended deployment overseas.

This metaphor of the team as a military unit continually resurfaced to explain other situations and employment experiences throughout my time at the *America's Army* game development studios. But it was a metaphor that had some grounding in real experiences as well, for many on the development team had trained together as a military unit when the army sent them to boot camp.

As it turned out, so many people were dressed in army combat uniforms on my first day of fieldwork because about one third of the developers—one woman and twelve men—had freshly returned from a voluntary five-day job-related excursion to Fort Jackson's Army Training Center (Hamacher 2007). Along with employees from other Army Game Project offices they underwent five days of "mini Basic Combat Training," otherwise known as "mini-BCT." During this short period of time they endured many of the same ordeals of resocialization as new entries to boot camp—buzz cuts, obstacle courses, pushups, cafeteria lines, weapons training, and obnoxious drill sergeants. They were assigned to squads, slept in barracks, and were issued their own equipment and uniforms, complete with an *America's Army* arm patch. Describing it later, one participant claimed, "The first day was one of the worst days of my life" (see fig. 17).

This ordeal had many purposes. At its core it was intended to give the game developers an experiential taste of boot camp for the purposes of integrating their new familiarity with army life into the video game. Many developers approached the event as an opportunity to build their professional skills as artists, sound technicians, level designers, programmers, and producers. Developers indicated that their mini-BCT experiences aided in the creation of an introductory framing segment of *America's Army 3* involving a virtual boot camp where users learn how to play by navigating an obstacle course, completing weapons familiarization, and running through a live-fire shoothouse. In this way the developers' experiences at mini-BCT came to be portrayed as a kind of halfway mark in a referential sequence pointing from the virtual boot camp of the game to the mini–boot camp of the game developers, to the "true" boot camp of the enlisted army soldier.

The army intended the in-game representations of boot camp to serve as an artificial placeholder for the real army boot camp. I would contend, however, that the representational process of *America's Army* is much more complex than this. I prefer to think of the game as part of a hyperrealistic narrative of what the army desires itself to be, a narrative that *produces*, rather than reflects, realities (Baudrillard 1994, 6). This means that *America's Army*, in a sense, precedes that which it represents, in much the same way that the contemporary boot camp experiences of many new army enlistees are preceded by an abundance of narratives (i.e., virtual boot camp experiences) populating the military entertainment culture industry.

In emphasizing the "truth" of the game's representational fidelity, press releases claimed the game as a "virtual test drive" of the army and that it is "as close to being in the Army as you can get without enlisting."[4] Tag lines for the game also revealed this rhetorical vice quite succinctly, declaring that "*America's Army* is a game like no other, because of its detailed level of authenticity" and that the game, although mostly created by subcontracted civilian developers, was "Designed, Developed, and Deployed by the U.S. Army."[5]

The army was quick to advertise the fact that it had sent its game developers to boot camp, enlisting them as virtual soldiers. The mini-BCT event was used for marketing to generate hype among video game players prior to the release of *America's Army 3* in June of 2009. The *America's Army* marketing agency put together a video and photos of the event, taking on-site film recordings and interspersing it with retrospective interviews of developers and video game footage.[6] Accompanying text to the video at the *America's Army* Facebook page hailed the game's authenticity, made all the more legitimate because of the mini-BCT experience: "What makes AA3 the most authentic military game ever? Developers actually go through Army basic training. See how they became Army Strong at Fort Jackson, South Carolina, and how their experiences make AA3 a game like no other in the world."[7] Two developers blogged about their experiences at mini-BCT, which they extensively described in online forums at americasarmy.com.[8] Short video teasers with various developers enabled fans to take behind-the-scenes looks at the work and offices of the development team. And, adhering to a promotional language of realism, a press release for *America's Army 3* advertised how its developers became transfigured into the role of a soldier, implying that players can also undergo a similar transformation through the game: "Nobody knows military simulations like the world's premier land force, the United States Army. So, when the Army began making the *America's Army* game to provide civilians with insights on Soldiering from the barracks to the battlefields, it sent its talented development team to experience Army training just as a new recruit would. The developers crawled through obstacle courses, fired weapons, observed paratrooper instruction, and participated in a variety of training exercises with elite combat units, all so that you could virtually experience Soldiering in the most realistic way possible."[9]

Despite the unexpected physical intensity of the mini-BCT experience, nearly all of the developers who attended the event remembered it as an occasion that contributed to their personal growth and understanding of the army. One developer wrote on the *America's Army* online forums that he and other coworkers "were yelled at, chided, [and] pushed beyond our physical and mental limitations, but came out all the stronger for it in the end because we endured."[10] After his return to the office another developer told some colleagues, "It has changed me. I don't know if for good or bad, but it has changed me." The only woman from the California office to attend described her experience as being "really moving, even though it wasn't the full blown experience. [It was] as much of a taste as you really can get without actually being in the army. I would never have opted to do it, knowing what I know now [about how difficult it was], but I'm glad that I did. I wasn't going to be the only person on the team that quit. Being a female, being a woman drives a lot of decisions that I make [in regards to my work]."

Often, these personal reasons for attending accompanied professional ones. This was the case with one producer (from another Army Game Project office) who stated that "the short answer as to why *I* want to go and do it is that I'm about to turn forty and I'd really like to know if I can handle it." He went on to articulate why he thought the army sent the game developers, telling me that "they believe the more we know about what it takes to turn civilians into soldiers the better we will be able to depict that in the things that we build. I think also that the more we know about tactics, techniques, trainings, and procedures, the more lifelike we can build scenarios, and the more effective we can be."

As this producer implied, "turning civilians into soldiers" no longer happens solely in the institution of the military; it has become a process that happens during the everyday life of media consumers in the United States. Nearly every American has become a willing, unwilling, or unwitting consumer of war and a participant in the national mediated narratives of war that are part of the "military normal" (Lutz 2009). "Soft sells" such as *America's Army*, the VAE, and the AEC further contribute to production of this militarized subjectivity by adding the dimension of interactivity and the veneer of user agency. By relying on user-generated interest in and discovery of the army through the game, *America's Army* material online, and public venues like the VAE and AEC, the messages of *America's Army*, which might be dismissed as heavy-handed statist propaganda in other contexts, instead morph into "impressions," which can be readily accepted. Such processes of subjectification, which originate from institutions but operate as if they derive from individual motives, exemplify how power capitalizes on the ostensibly liberatory nature of social media, interactive entertainment, and networks of information sharing in the early twenty-first century.

The marketing and media efforts of mini-BCT capitalized on the affective performance of the game developers as soldiers. This figure worked to translate and reconfigure military power to gamers, suggesting to players that they also can possess the knowledge and expertise that was imparted to the game developers by the army—either by participating within the liminal space of the game, or better yet, enlisting and joining the army. Through these diverse methods, both developers and players of *America's Army* became virtual soldiers.

Selfless Service during Crunch Time

Following the developers' return to California, stories of mini-BCT continued to periodically effervesce in conversations, and the experience became one of many in the folklore of *America's Army* game development. For some it was a high point in their employment at the studio, for in the year following mini-BCT the team went through difficult times. There was a general lack of direction and vision, both internally and externally, as to what the new *America's Army 3* was supposed to be like. One root of these problems was a frustrating and convoluted system of military contracting and subcontracting that separated the development team from much army institutional support. In an arrangement that was confusing at best, the team's offices near Berkeley communicated with a variety of other offices across the United States. In name the development team worked for a private company. This company was contracted to develop *America's Army* by another large private military contractor, SAIC, which was, in turn, contracted by the U.S. government. But there was minimal contact between the game developers and these private employers; instead their customers, the U.S. Army and the U.S. government, oversaw the majority of project operations from offices in Alabama and at West Point.

This arrangement led to many difficulties. Nearly everyone in the office felt that the government management of the project from the Alabama offices was incompetent. The demands placed on them to perform their work, they felt, did not match the amount of monetary and institutional support that trickled down to the office after the prime contractor (SAIC) and the subcontractor (DCS) had taken a substantial portion of operational funding allocated to the development of the game. Often, they felt, the team became a scapegoat for problems that originated elsewhere. In one exchange during an interview with a developer named Benjamin, I asked what he felt about the project management outside of the team in regards to their understanding of the process of game development. I had overheard Wardynski exclaim during a visit to the studio that the game "industry is full of flakes," and I wanted to see if this was a prevailing opinion among Army Game Project members in the military and government: "I don't think they have any idea. It doesn't seem uncommon, this sort of understanding as to what actually goes into producing this stuff. These people just don't understand how [games] are made. [Allen: Do you think they are like, 'They just play all the time'?] Yeah, 'They're just messing around!' They don't really understand what goes into it all and the nuts and bolts—how much work is actually required." The development process, he told me, was seen as a kind of mystified, occult work from the perspective of these outsiders: "The end product is all this fun, all this cool stuff, so for them it's just this 'magic' that happens behind the scenes and for them it must seem rad doing it because playing the product is fun. I don't think they have any idea as to how tenuous everything still is."

Following a series of employment shakeups that eliminated most of the experienced members of the development team, those remaining became demoralized and doubtful of their own job security. This created a considerable level of hostility toward project management, but also a closer level of camaraderie among team members. "No one is here out of loyalty to the product at this point," Benjamin went on to tell me, "Everyone who is still here after all of those firings took place is here out of loyalty to each other and to the people who got let go. We're not going to disgrace their efforts that they put in to trying to get this game out the door; we're not going to screw over each other by abandoning this project so that people don't have the credit to put on their resumes." When this came to a head near the lowest point of the 2009 economic recession, Walker assessed the team's situation in terms of troop morale:

All of us—the team as a whole—would feel much, much better if we could see a year into the future. But that is a well-guarded secret. That is a problem, a *huge* problem. It is a problem with our management; it is a problem with the army. It is a problem that will have to be solved if they want to continue to do this, because it is *horrible* for morale. [. . .] If they don't want people to continue to look for jobs all day long, then they need to make them feel like they are going to be taken care of in the future, and that is something that is *severely* lacking.

When it was useful to their purposes, members of the army sought to militarize this discontent by continuing to project to the subcontracted development team a sense of inclusion within the larger organization of the army. In a team meeting, a visiting senior officer sought to encourage the overworked and understaffed office as they entered "crunch time" a few months prior to the release of *America's Army 3*. Speaking to them as if they were soldiers and framing their work in terms of "selfless service," one of the seven core army values, he told them, "Thank you for putting up with the drama [. . .] but you can't quit, because you represent̶ ̶ ̶ ̶ ̶ ̶'on that doesn't quit. This country wouldn't be

here if the organization that you represent had a quitter's attitude. I don't care who pays you, you work for the army. You're going to have to be like the Special Forces and do more with less. You have the Special Forces mentality. [. . .] Everybody wanted to have a piece of the bad guy after 9/11. You guys are serving the war effort in a huge way."

While the senior officer's ploy did not appear to work in terms of motivating the developers, his words were not visibly dismissed for their reliance on cheap platitudes and patriotic appeals. The developers took pride in their work, and most were pleased to be creating something both noncommercial and for the army. For this reason, and despite their disagreements with individuals at the project management level, the office's orientation in regards to "big Army" at the institutional level was a positive one. But the pressing needs of job security, more competitive salaries, and better benefits—in addition to receiving much-needed resources to ensure the timely release of *America's Army 3*—were on the minds of nearly everyone at the time. When these issues were mentioned to the officer he dismissed them, telling the team, "That's not a big problem, I think." But some developers persisted, petitioning to him, "We've lost talent, and can't attract talent because we can't pay competitively. We want to continue to work for the project, but [management] has screwed us." Choosing not to take into account these realities, the officer instead interpreted this as a threat and asked the team, "Is this a 'let's have a walkout' kind of problem?"

In eliding the fact that the game developers were laborers by implying that they were developing the game purely for patriotic reasons to help "get a piece of the bad guy," the senior officer recreated the situation of many soldiers who join the military for primarily economic reasons but nevertheless feel compelled to speak of their enlistment in terms of national service. The language of selfless service mystifies the economic reasons underlying employment in the military and by military contractors. Anthropologist Andrew Bickford writes that "if we think of the U.S. military as a labor market, and its soldiers as workers, these are people who find themselves in coercive and exploitative situations [that] can compel soldiers to fight and soldier on; it is a form of labor rationalization . . . that ultimately does little for the soldier" (2009, 151). His description of soldier labor applies to that of the game developers' work as well, for these virtual soldiers were essentially asked to continue projecting the affective qualities of a soldier by pushing on through crunch time in the service of their nation.

Crunch time abruptly ended on June 17, 2009, when the completed *America's Army* 3 was released to the public for free download. At the end of the workday I accompanied the developers to their favorite Emeryville bar for a celebration. The next morning we arrived in the studio to find the usually dark office space brightly lit and all computers locked. On that day all but a handful of employees were laid off without prior warning and the Emeryville development office was shut down. Wardynski himself did not make an appearance, and instead opted to send his deputy Maj. Mike Marty, who executed the layoffs as if disciplining unruly soldiers. Referring to the move as a "consolidation," a representative from the SED told reporters that the layoffs "will allow us to gain efficiencies between our public and government applications" (Faylor 2009; McWhertor 2009). According to other unofficial sources, though, there simply was not any money for the program. Due to the economic downturn enlistment in the army was up, and existing funds reportedly had to be used simply for "keeping the patient alive."[11] Even though *America's Army* had generated a considerable number of recruiting achievements and publicity over the years, such novel efforts had simply become less of an immediate fiscal priority. I was told that funding for the Army Game Project, typically cobbled together from previously reliable annual budget surpluses from a variety of army organizations, had materialized only at 15 percent of previous levels.

Largely due to preexisting external issues that were beyond the control of the California studio, the free game was critically broken and essentially unplayable for several weeks after its release. The executive producer Mike Bode, along with two others, stayed on the team to help patch these issues through the summer of 2009, but the efforts of only three individuals were not enough. The free game quickly lost popularity and users. Frustrated players, many of them soldiers and veterans, had waited expectantly for months to download it, and they naturally equated news of the layoffs as retribution for the broken *America's Army* 3. In an angry retort to players' mounting criticisms of the game and its developers, one of the former developers posted a comment (quickly deleted by forum moderators) at the americasarmy.com forums. He implored fans "to imagine trying to build a game with an impossible deadline, steadily declining workforce (via firings), a hiring freeze, constantly being fed misinformation, having the 'higher ups' completely ignore your weekly plea for either a) more time, or b) more manpower, working a ton of unpaid overtime, pouring your heart and soul into a misadventure only to have the uniformed community scoff at you for uncontrollable variables . . . *right* when you've just lost your job."[12]

On the same day as the layoffs, a box of *America's Army 3* shirts, which they had ordered and paid for themselves, arrived. One developer told anybody around who was there to listen, "They should make us a shirt that says, 'I made a video game and all I got was this shirt.'" Through multiple channels it had become painfully and abruptly clear to all of the developers that despite the similitude of their experiences to actual soldiers, they were, in the end, ex-employees of a subcontractor to a contractor to the U.S. military. "The army takes care of its own" was a phrase that was ironically repeated during the days following the layoffs. They had always understood that they were not a part of "its own," and that, anyway, the army rarely adequately takes care of even "its own" veterans (see Rieman interview, chapter 3). But there was an expressive bitterness in their words that seemed unusually high, even for freshly laid-off workers. A great deal of this rancor derived from a growing realization that the closest parallel between their experiences and the experiences of many U.S. soldiers was, ultimately, that they ended up feeling forgotten, unappreciated, and discarded by the military (see fig. 18).

Much ado could be made about the uniqueness of the developers' situation. But my primary point in describing their experiences here has not been to elicit sympathy for them or to show how their situation was anomalous. The abrupt joblessness of the developers was unfortunately not an abnormality, especially in California during June of 2009, when the state unemployment rate was fast approaching 12 percent (U.S. Bureau of Labor Statistics 2010). Fluctuation in the video game labor market, punctuated by mass layoffs, has been an industry norm and post-Fordist principle for years.

My purpose, instead, has been to explain how the circumstances of the developers might illuminate general trends in the militarization of popular culture in the United States. The enlistment of the developers' labor to perform as virtual soldiers highlights a pervasive mobilization of the culture industry and the cognitive capacities of its laborers as vehicles of war. The corporatization of the military and the militarization of corporations are underlying engines of this trend, which is only accelerating. As more private mercenaries become employed in U.S. foreign occupations and counterterrorism attempts; as more businesses become contracted through Pentagon funding initiatives; as the capabilities of digital technologies increase the immersive qualities of military entertainment; and as social scientists weaponize culture and ethnography (Price 2011; Whitehead and Finnström 2013), new forms of virtual soldiering will emerge. It might, sooner or later, behoove everyone to ask themselves, "How am I a virtual soldier?"

Epilogue: The Godfather

I was confronted with this question for the first time one month prior to the layoffs when I joined the developers at the 2009 Game Developers Conference, where they were giving exclusive previews to *America's Army 3* to video game journalists in a back room of the W Hotel. Wardynski was talking with me and some SED government employees when he turned to me to ask, "Have you ever seen the *Godfather* movies?"

"Yes," I replied.

"You're a good guy, right?" he asked. "Well, I hope you are because otherwise I'll have to take care of you and kill you."

"I didn't think that sort of thing was supposed to be something the army does, sir," I rejoined.

"I'm not talking about the army," he clarified, "I'm talking about me." All I could do was smile falsely, unsure about how exactly to interpret that statement. I remembered another flippant (but at the same time fully serious) comment that the Army Experience Center's Pentagon program director, Maj. Larry Dillard, told me in Philadelphia: "Tell the truth—don't say bad things." As if the "truth" is that which only reflects the "good" aspects of the U.S. Army.

What does one do as an ethnographer when a full-bird colonel, your principal research subject, threatens you? Granted, the context was in joking hyperbole, during a casual hallway conversation with other Army Game Project executives, but I had been around Wardynski and those who knew him long enough to understand that his threats, however metaphorical and offhand, were not to be taken lightly. As I have described above, Wardynski liked to refer to himself as "the Godfather," and some developers delighted in this practice as well, comparing him to both Francis Ford Coppola's Godfather character and another colonel figure nicknamed "Godfather" in Evan Wright's book (2004) and HBO miniseries *Generation Kill* (2008). Wardynski had at times channeled a mafia ruthlessness in his business and employment practices—mostly due to fiscal and institutional necessity, but perhaps sometimes, developers felt, simultaneously due to vendetta as a "price for failure."

I have often returned to this conversation to wonder about what Wardynski was trying to achieve in making the comparison between the Army Game Project and the Mafia (and, by extension, my questioned loyalty to the Army Game Project "family"). I have also pondered why he allowed the research I was doing to even be carried out in the first place if he felt that such a metaphorical threat was needed. The most direct answer I ever received from him was that, as an academic and a military academy officer, he felt that it was his obligation to support research in whatever manner was plausible. I do not have any reason to doubt the sincerity of this sentiment, as Wardynski has demonstrated a willingness not only to be open to new ideas but also to act on them. Now, however, I understand that through his Mafia-couched threat, Wardynski was anticipating my witnessing of the already-planned layoffs and my recording of the ugly fallout of that event. He had given me research access in 2006, when the Army Game Project was at its apex in funding and scope, but by the time of this encounter the project was underfunded and crashing, along with the global economy. In 2006 he had not foreseen that I would witness the unravelling of the project, and he was now hedging against what I might write about all of that.

I view my exceptional access to the Army Game Project—an institution competing for funding and legitimacy—as being somewhat politically motivated, due to the potential utility my research and presence afforded Wardynski and others in several areas. I do not think that it is unreasonable to consider that I was, in fact, a "spy" of sorts in my ability to travel from institution to institution on a regular basis. I am not naïve enough to think that the heavy hindrances of work politics did not cloud my relationships with individuals. Some game developers became friends, and I inevitably came to see things from their point of view on a more regular basis. I do, however, think that the veneer of objectivity that was afforded me as an outside academic helped me ask difficult questions more easily and access information that was unavailable to those typically embedded in the Army Game Project work environments. Although I never conveyed any information that would compromise my first obligation to protect the individuals among whom I was conducting research, I was honest when others asked my opinion on the project and the general atmosphere of various offices. My interviews often felt like a much-needed chance for people to discuss their work frustrations and aspirations.

Many people compared me to embedded reporters, or regular journalists, and of all the institutions I came into contact with, the SED was by far the wariest of my presence—both within their building at Redstone Arsenal and anywhere else—and the most circumspect in their communication. Had it not been for Wardynski's blessing, I do not think that I would have ever set foot on base in Alabama. Other companies, like Ignited, seemed appreciative that an academic was attempting to take their product on its own terms, rather than beginning with criticisms, while others—including Wardynski himself—seemed to view me as a chance for good PR, another way to get their "message" out. The company of an external academic researcher perhaps added a small amount of legitimacy within military and government circles to the project, but I do not fool myself in thinking that I was generally seen as adding value to the Army Game Project by merely being present. In these different forms of inclusion within the institutional structure of the Army Game Project, I came to understand that my own labor as an anthropologist was being drawn on in some small way; like the developers I was researching, I also was enlisted as a virtual soldier.

In this book I have argued that virtual soldiering is central to how contemporary U.S. military institutions exert power over individuals. Virtual soldiering is a form of immaterial labor that does not require a person to be an actual soldier or even to have the desire to become one in the future. The developers of *America's Army* and I were both enlisted as virtual soldiers in some regard, but the entire franchise of *America's Army* did so in myriad other ways for different individuals: at the Virtual Army Experience and the Army Experience Center; through the Real Hero stories like that of Tommy Rieman, juxtaposed against the enemy other of *America's Army*; through Wardynski's careful positioning of the game in the midst of social and political controversy around violence in games; through staged invasions by actual soldiers of video game conferences in Los Angeles; and in comic books or through the experiences of players like PJ, described in the opening section of this book. In all of these contexts, virtual soldiering happens.

Virtual soldiering happens in other contexts that go well beyond one game, too. The years since the "invasion of E3" that debuted *America's Army* at the Los Angeles Convention Center in 2002 have witnessed a rapid evolution in military entertainment; entire sectors of the economy, forms of labor, methods of entertainment, and networks of information are now quantitatively and qualitatively more militarized. *America's Army* marks a significant chapter in the militarization of American culture, which has been happening since at least the 1950s. From a historical perspective, the networks of power and production of *America's Army* examined here should not be viewed as an exception or a curious anomaly, but as a harbinger of more advanced recruitment and advertising methods—not only for the military, but also for corporations and products. Games and virtual interfaces are increasingly becoming used for recruitment, education, training, and weapons development. They are being used to mediate and carry out actual fighting just as they are also commonly being used as vehicles for entertainment, socialization, and even news and information. As these technologies of the visual continue to blend what we think of as being virtual and actual experience, virtual mediation will become more pronounced, not only in everyday entertainment and socialization but also in war and our consumption of it.

It is unclear how much of a role *America's Army* will continue to have in this process, though. After the closing of the California studio the development of the game was fully absorbed by the SED and production moved entirely to Alabama. Past executive producer Phil DeLuca predicted this happening two months before the layoffs, indicating to me that the project was "positioned well for the SED to take it over. It is a government entity and it's got a lot of inertia. And it's not fast-moving inertia. They like to control things, and anything that's outside of their direct control they'll eventually pull in. They're slow, they're the starfish, so they'll just keep on pulling until that clam gives it up." Though still operational in 2016, the project has had to cut many of its ventures, including the Virtual Army Experience, which ironically won two Effie awards in the preeminent marketing awards ceremony held two weeks prior to the project-wide layoffs in 2009. The VAE won a gold in the "government/institutional/recruitment" category and a silver for "brand experience," and the army and Ignited also won a bronze Effie for the Army Experience Center in the "brand experience" category in 2010. Now renamed the Army Game Studio within the SED, *America's Army 3* continues to be minimally supported, with software bug fixes and updated versions released on a semiregular basis. In 2010 Wardynski retired from the army to become the superintendent of Huntsville, Alabama, city schools, a relocation that indicates that his ongoing involvement in the project is not out of the question, especially given the ties between educational and military institutions discussed in chapter five.

In 2013 the SED sought to reignite enthusiasm for *America's Army* with the release of a new game, *America's Army: Proving Grounds*, largely based on *America's Army 3*, but with a more simplified and streamlined play style. Czervenia persisted as a menace in both the game and the *America's Army Graphic Novel* series, which continues to be published as of 2016 as free digital downloads for tablets, smartphones, and PCs. Over the years since the publication of *America's Army 3* in 2009, the Czervenian enemy has come to more explicitly parallel a Russian enemy through its visual iconography, a scare-tactic development that is not without consequence, given the ongoing proxy wars between Putin's Russia and the United States–led NATO alliance in both Syria and Ukraine. This evolving unreal enemy of *America's Army* is a far cry from the vaguely Middle Eastern ski-masked terrorist enemy of the original 2002 game. Though such representations are a reflection of current geopolitical conditions, they also discipline the expectations of media users to match possible future realities of war.

The next American war—whenever or wherever it may be—will no doubt involve the enlistment of virtual soldiers drilled in other, similar ways that simultaneously shape expectations of war and attune bodies to future military institutional needs for the labor of war (see also Parikka 2014). Just as the skills of drone pilots have been honed through games and simulations, perhaps new forms of virtual soldiering are already being shaped by the rapidly developing technologies of the smartphone, augmented reality, and virtual reality. These technologies of the digital certainly work toward other ends, which may come to mitigate and reduce militarized violence and ways of understanding an increasingly interconnected world. For the near future, however, game and simulation technologies will continue to take center stage in the process of training a "reserve army" of virtual soldiers, the everyday consumers and users of media who are America's digital army.

Notes

1. America's Digital Army

1. All given names that initially appear without a surname are pseudonyms. Names that are accompanied by a surname are the actual names of individuals. See note 6 for further naming details and conventions.
2. See Stahl 2007 for an insightful investigation about the news media portrayal of Iraq and Saddam Hussein prior to and during the first several years of the Iraq occupation.
3. See http://pc.gamespy.com/pc/americas-army/951010p1.html, accessed May 3, 2014.
4. Personal email from Mike Zyda to the author, dated May 12, 2006.
5. When I write of "institutional power" I understand it to mean biopower and disciplinary power as formulated in the Foucauldian tradition.
6. Note on interviews: All names of interviewees with surnames are their actual names. In most cases these are individuals who are already identifiable due to being in a more public position. More often, however, I have anonymized interviewee names to protect their identity as employees, sometimes creating composites that combine two or more individuals. Anonymized interviewee names are always first names, if a name appears at all. All quoted interview material was either audio-recorded and transcribed or recorded directly in my fieldnotes. Everything within quotes is verbatim dialogue, although I have taken the liberty to edit redundancies, small grammatical issues, and verbal tics that would affect the ease of reading. For quoted interviews I follow *Chicago Manual of Style* suggestions for use of ellipses. Ellipses inside brackets ([. . .]) indicate that a section of the interview has been deleted for the sake of readability. Regular ellipses within quoted interviews (. . .) indicate a pause in the conversation or an incomplete or interrupted thought.
7. Der Derian 2001; Hardt and Negri 2000, 2004; Lenoir 2000; Lutz 2006; and Turse 2008 are among some prominent examples to use these various phrasings, all of which attempt to describe the same phenomenon.

2. *The Art of Persuasion*

1. Formerly called STRICOM (Simulation Training and Instrumentation Command).
2. http://www.linkedin.com/in/caseywardynski, accessed November 13, 2015.
3. http://www.linkedin.com/in/caseywardynski, accessed November 13, 2015.
4. The books that academics keep communicate their research orientation and interests, and this was true for Wardynski. His office shelves prominently displayed volumes such as *The Leadership Secrets of Colin Powell* (Harari 2002); *Freakonomics: A Rogue Economist Explores the Hidden Side of Everything* (Levitt and Dubner 2005); *Changing the Game: How Video Games Are Transforming the Future of Business* (Edery and Mollick 2009); *The 9/11 Commission Report* (National Commission on Terrorist Attacks 2004); *Going to the Mines to Look for Diamonds: Experimenting with Military Recruiting Stations in Malls* (Fricker and Fair 2003); and movies such as *Gettysburg, Braveheart, Wall Street, Trading Places, Boiler Room, Stripes* (a professed favorite of his), and *We Were Soldiers*.
5. From his perspective, some of these efforts would likely include the Department of Defense–funded Institute for Creative Technologies' games *Full Spectrum Warrior* (Pandemic Studios 2004) and *Full Spectrum Warrior: Ten Hammers* (Pandemic Studios 2006), as well as the navy game *Strike and Retrieve* (U.S. Navy 2005). Although it has proven in the intervening years since this interview to be more successful than *America's Army* in terms of military institutionalization, Wardynski is likely also referring to army training simulation competitor PEO-STRI and their contracts for Bohemia Interactive's *Virtual Battlespace* simulation franchise (*VBS2* and *VBS3*), the official training simulations for the U.S. Army.
6. Through findings discovered through Freedom of Information Act requests, *Gamespot* reports that the total cost for the Army Game Project between 2000 and 2009 was $32.8 million, averaging $3.28 million per year during the game's first ten years of development (Sinclair 2009).
7. Steam is the leader in content distribution for digital download of PC games and is the most popular method of accessing *America's Army 3*. Fileplanet predates Steam and is another method of downloading digital game content.
8. Public relations documents written by Wardynski (2009) for selling the game's legitimacy to military and government representatives draw explicitly on literature about persuasive technologies and behavioral economics, which was Wardynski's PhD specialization.
9. Fogg's book (2003) directly influenced Wardynski's approach to games as tools for persuasion.

10. See the *America's Army 3* FAQ statement, page 30: http://aa3.americas
army.com/documents/AA3_Knowledge_Center_FAQ.pdf, accessed July 2,
2014.

11. This is a summary of a lengthy text. Title 10, Chapter 307, § 3062 (U.S.
Congress 2011) provides for "an Army that is capable, in conjunction with
other armed forces, of . . . overcoming any nations responsible for
aggressive acts that imperil the peace and security of the United
States. . . . [T]he Army . . . includes land combat and service forces and
such aviation and water transport as may be organic therein."

12. See http://www.unr.edu/art/delappe/gaming/dead_in_iraq/dead_in
_iraq%20jpegs.html, accessed July 4, 2014.

13. See http://www.americasdiplomat.com/, accessed February 16, 2012.
Page no longer available online. See http://nytimes-se.com/todays-paper
/NYTimes-SE.pdf, accessed July 4, 2014, for a PDF copy of a spoof of the
New York Times written by DeLappe that references the "America's
Diplomat" project.

3. The Virtual and the Real

1. Here I draw on Jean Baudrillard's thought regarding hyperreality and
"the precession of simulacra," in which the simulation of an event
precedes the event itself and, paradoxically, acts as the means of bringing
about the event (1994; see also Eco 1986).

2. PJ's combat experiences in chapter 1 take place within Czervenia.

3. "The only good Czervo is a dead Czervo," echoing pejorative statements
made about American Indians (Meider 1993) and other dehumanizing
racial slurs used against Japanese, Vietnamese, Korean, and other soldiers
of various ethnicities who have been enemies of the American military at
one point or another. "Czervo" later became a regularly used word in the
America's Army Graphic Novel series.

4. Axe products have been advertised in military-themed video games such
as *Splinter Cell: Chaos Theory* and *Ghost Recon: Advanced Warfighter* in
addition to Axe's very own series of browser-based marketing games, no
longer available online, that were loaded with male heterosexual fantasy.
Such symbiotic and networked relationships between various products
and industries—deodorants, video games, the military—are usually not
recognized by most individuals. The ROTC cadet whose idea it was to use
Axe body spray as a U.S. Army–issued weapon, however, made this
connection.

5. Simons paints a different picture of Fayetteville and Fort Bragg than Lutz,
one that is exclusively from the point of view of the Special Forces soldiers

with whom she conducted fieldwork. She describes how a growing emphasis on missions involving "direct action" (i.e., combat) is changing the type of soldier interested in joining the Special Forces. This emphasis, Simons laments, is at the expense of the other three areas of Special Forces operations that do not involve direct combat but nevertheless make up the overwhelming bulk of Special Forces missions: unconventional warfare, foreign internal defense, and special reconnaissance. The iterations of *America's Army: Special Forces* (versions 2.0 to 2.8.4) emphasize direct action and reinforce this trend.

6. One curator of the *Bang the Machine* exhibition, Stanford video game historian and media collections curator Henry Lowood, further detailed this event to me in a personal interview, November 2008.

7. See PJ's introductory section at the beginning of the book for a description of how in-game combat life-saving mechanics work in *America's Army 3*.

8. One major requirement for becoming a Real Hero was distinction through medals. Every Real Hero had been awarded either a Bronze Star with "V" Device, a Silver Star, or the Distinguished Service Cross.

9. Originally at http://www.americasarmy.com/realheroes/index.php?id ¼44&view¼bio, accessed April 6, 2010 (content no longer available). Wolford's profile and Real Hero video biography are republished at the time of writing at http://www.liveleak.com/view?i=dea_1221257938, accessed November 16, 2015.

10. For a transcript of the speech, see http://www.foxnews.com/story /2007/01/23/transcript-presidnt-bush-state-union-address/, accessed November 18, 2015. Rieman was also awarded the Purple Heart, which is given to soldiers who experience physical injury sustained by combat. Its omission here is telling.

11. Lutz (2001) details the problematic recurrence and history of the idea of soldiers as "super citizens" whose labor is privileged above other forms of work.

4. The Full-Spectrum Soft Sell

1. Marcus is conflating two separate marine corps commercials, one involving a man climbing a cliff (https://www.youtube.com/watch?v=X SBnJ7H-CAc, accessed December 6, 2015) and another involving fighting a dragon (https://www.youtube.com/watch?v=62tnJtLBQzQ, accessed December 6, 2015).

2. The AEC was not a formal part of the Army Game Project and was

managed out of the Pentagon. The VAE was managed by both OEMA and the SED in Alabama. Ignited was responsible for the concept and implantation of both, and *America's Army* was the core game software underlying both.

3. At the time of this interview Long was co-CEO of Seattle-based Zombie Studios, one of the contracting software developers of the VAE along the *America's Army* California-based game development team.

4. See Wardynski's comments about ESRB ratings and *America's Army* products in my chapter 2 interview. The issue of whether the VAE was age-appropriate continued to be a controversy throughout its existence and came to a head at several occasions (e.g., Rutledge 2008).

5. For the teaser most typically played at the VAE, see https://www.youtube .com/watch?v=JU19Bsw-rss#t=21, accessed November 18, 2015.

6. In gamer jargon "respawn" refers to the gaming convention in which a player's avatar returns to life after being defeated; "god mode" refers to a state in video games in which the player's avatar is invulnerable to damage.

7. Personal fieldnotes. See also http://www.youtube.com/watch?v=B51 abXkmN I&feature=related, accessed November 18, 2015, for similar phrasings. Similar claims were made by *America's Army* game developers about their experiences at mini Basic Combat Training.

8. For a representative example of a Real Hero video that was shown at the VAE, see https://www.youtube.com/watch?v=2ivHf5OwmGA#t=14, accessed July 21, 2014.

9. http://www.americasarmy.com/realheroes/index.php?id=3&view=bio, accessed June 23, 2011 (no longer available online).

10. For Rieman's Real Hero video, see https://www.youtube.com/watch?v =30rVaa4VdRY, accessed July 22, 2014.

11. The AEC was run through the chief marketing officer for the army's office, which was organized under the Office of the Assistant Secretary of the Army (Manpower and Reserve Affairs), Marketing and Recruiting division.

12. See, for example, Carroll 2009 (CNN video report); Leland 2009 (*New York Times* article); Williams 2009 (*NBC Nightly News* report); and Denvir 2008 (*Free Speech Radio News*).

13. Amy Lindstrom, Ignited public relations representative, personal interview.

14. Maj. Larry Dillard, personal interview; Al Flood, personal interview.

15. PHASE 4 funding organization, the Heinz Foundation, confusingly writes, "Fifty-five percent of PHASE 4's students are referred from school districts where over forty-one percent of the students are from low income

families." http://www.heinz.org/Interior.aspx?id=417&view=entry&eid=566, accessed July 28, 2014.

16. http://www.heinz.org/Interior.aspx?id=417&view=entry&eid=566, accessed July 28, 2014.

17. Flood was also a career army officer as a helicopter pilot, generals' aide, and ROTC instructor. At about the same time as the AEC's permanent—and planned—closure, Casey Wardynski likewise retired from the army and became the superintendent of the Huntsville, Alabama, city schools in June 2010.

18. This parallels the militarization of other activist movements described by Enloe (2000, 14–34).

19. "Killing in the Name" has also been used by the military as a sonic instrument of torture on some of the detainees at Guantanamo Bay. Playing the music at high volumes for indefinite periods of time is a practice antithetical to all messages within the music itself and demonstrates how any material or immaterial thing can be militarized. Of this practice, Rage Against the Machine guitarist Tom Morello is quoted to have said, "The fact that music I helped create was used in crimes against humanity sickens me" (BBC 2009).

5. The Military Entertainment Complex

1. The most prominent examples include Chaplin and Ruby 2005, 192–221; Crogan 2011; Der Derian 2001, 2003; Gray 1997, 2003, 2005; Halter 2006, 175–238; Herz 1999, 197–213; Kline et al. 2003, 179–83; Lenoir 2000, 2003; Lenoir and Lowood 2005; Li 2003; Mead 2013; Nieborg 2005, 2009; Pasanen 2009; Stahl 2010, 91–112.

2. Anonymous quoted material in this chapter derives from many interviews that I conducted with *America's Army* developers over the course of one and a half years, between November 2007 and April 2009.

3. See http://ict.usc.edu/about/pdf-overviews/, accessed May 1, 2014, for an overview list of ICT projects. Gonzalez (2012) further details similar "cultural awareness" exercises for military training.

4. I base this history of *America's Army* on accounts described in Chaplin and Ruby (2005), Halter (2006), and Zyda et al. (2005), as well as my own interviews and email communication with Zyda, Wardynski, and approximately ten other *America's Army* employees.

5. Orson Scott Card's book *Ender's Game* (1991) also was an inspirational text to other closely associated individuals in the military gaming field (Chaplin and Ruby 2005, 195). In the book a young boy's skills at directing

apparently simulated space battles prove to be the strategic edge in a war to save humanity against an alien bug-like species.

6. See http://hardforum.com/showthread.php?t=1428555, accessed November 30, 2015. The former developer continues, writing that "that's the short version of the story. The whole story could fill a book."

7. See http://www.sandia.gov/adaptive-training-systems/Fact%20Sheets /ATS%20FactSheet%20CogSys%20Sheet%2010-04-06%20edit.pdf, accessed November 30, 2015.

8. The Future Soldier Trainer (FST) and Future Soldier Training System (FSTS) were two separate products designed with the goal of reaching new enlistees, with the underlying theory that virtual engagement with new recruits reduces attrition. The Future Soldiers program has additionally implemented mobile Android and ios devices in its program. See http://www.futuresoldiers.com/training/index.jsp?contentId=fs_fsts, accessed June 4, 2014.

9. Zombie relied on military contracts to supplement its revenue from the commercial sector. *Future Force Company Commander* (F2C2), a simulation meant to depict a technologically savvy army-of-the-future, was one such contract that Zombie completed for the military contractor, SAIC. Zombie also played a significant role in outsourced development work for the Virtual Army Experience and *America's Army 3*.

10. The message read, in part: "In the early 1940s, Japan learned an important lesson—'let the sleeping giant lie.' We may not react swiftly, but when we do it's with unstoppable force. . . . The Army has partners that deal with cybercrime as a matter of course. These include not just various Army IT departments, but also the Department of Justice, the Secret Service, and the Federal Bureau of Investigations [*sic*]. . . . Allow me to speak directly to the bad guys for a moment: When you get banned, know that we know and have records showing you were doing something that's a violation of terms of service, breaks your EULA, and also happens to be against the law. We know who you are, and can track down where you play from. We have incontrovertible proof you did something illegal. The Army is angry, and we're coming for you." See http://www.unknown worlds.com/forums/lofiversion/index.php/t86439.html, accessed July 24, 2016.

11. One example, Bode said, was in simple activities, like riding in another person's car. A government employee "technically can't ride in my car or any other contractor's because that can be construed as giving him a favor. But I can ride in his car. So when we go to lunch, I can't treat him.

He can treat me. Weird stuff [that] can really impact your relationship with those people."

12. See http://archive.fortune.com/magazines/fortune/fortune500/2012 /full_list/201_300.html, accessed June 6, 2014.

13. See http://arcadeheroes.com/2007/07/20/americas-army-coming-to -arcades/, accessed June 8, 2014.

14. See http://www3.ausa.org/webint/DeptAUSANews.nsf/byid/PGRH-7N2 QQU, accessed June 8, 2014.

15. See http://www.army.mil/article/12589/, accessed November 30, 2015.

16. During my three visits to the SED, extremely tight security restrictions dictated that I be escorted at all times, including bathroom breaks, when inside any building. To enter Redstone Arsenal I had to undergo an extensive security check, and I often had to be picked up by project managers at the entrance to the base, about a fifteen-minute drive away from the SED. My visits consequently placed considerably more strain on the employees there than they did on employees in Emeryville. To further complicate both game development and fieldwork, a number of government firewalls designed to prevent cyberattacks acted as continual barriers to the development process of *America's Army*. Workers at the SED using government computers for the game, for example, could not download, access, or play their own game from the Internet at certain points in time.

17. Perforce revision control software, Adobe Flash, and Beast lighting software for games were three specific examples cited to me by developers.

18. This blog post has circulated throughout *America's Army* user forums since its original posting in 2005. See http://archive.forum.americasarmy .com/viewtopic.php?t=155861, accessed July 4, 2014; and http://battle tracker.com/forum/america-s-army-3-0-forums/america-s-army-3-0-dis cussion/p2676712-new-message-from-the-dev-s/, accessed July 4, 2014.

6. The Labor of Virtual Soldiers

1. For a survey of interactive industry employment norms at the time of the events described here, see http://www.gamecareerguide.com/features /416/the_game_industry_salary_survey_2007.php?page=1, accessed August 13, 2014.

2. Valve's *Team Fortress II* and *Left 4 Dead* were popular studio favorites.

3. See www.milspecmonkey.com, which designs and sells military gear and patches.

4. Such claims are also made for other Army Game Project products, like the Virtual Army Experience.

5. See, for example, http://forums.dmccaffer.co.uk/index.php?showtopic =2621, accessed August 15, 2014.

6. For the video, see https://www.youtube.com/watch?v=aY35d-lTVoY, accessed August 15, 2014; https://www.facebook.com/video/video.php ?v=209342018104, accessed August 17, 2014.

7. Text and video located at https://www.facebook.com/video/video.php ?v=209342018104, accessed November 20, 2015.

8. The blogs are no longer online but were originally available at http:// www.aa3.americasarmy.com/about/article.php?blogid=1, accessed March 1, 2010; and http://www.americasarmy.com/about/blogs.php ?blogid=2, accessed March 1, 2010.

9. http://www.goarmy.com/downloads/americas_army.jsp, accessed March 1, 2010.

10. The blog was originally posted at http://forum.americasarmy.com/view topic.php?t=269828, accessed November 13, 2009 (no longer available online).

11. As the SED project manager of *America's Army* two years later told me over the phone regarding the defunding of many previous Army Game Project projects, including that of the Emeryville studio, "It's political. It's all political." Another executive in the Army Game Project reported to me that "there was definitely mismanagement of funds" and that it was "a massive management failure" in not even having the money to work on the game after it was released.

12. For republications of the now deleted forum post, see http://www.game politics.com/2009/06/20/america039s-army-launches-new-version -sacks-developers-moves-hq, accessed August 15, 2014; http://www.game spot.com/forums/pc-mac-discussion-1000004/americas-army-develop er-explains-what-happend-26925250/, accessed August 15, 2014.

Glossary

> The military's preferred defense against civilian scrutiny: a mix of abbreviations, acronyms, and new concepts, all imaginatively arrayed on PowerPoint slides, leaving even a semiotician . . . in a state of slightly bewildered awe.
>
> JAMES DER DERIAN, *Virtuous War*

AA3: *America's Army 3*, released on June 17, 2009.

AAFA: *America's Army* Future Applications was located in Picatinny Arsenal, New Jersey.

AAGA: *America's Army* Government Applications, located at Virtual Heroes.

AAPA: *America's Army* Public Applications had offices in California located, in chronological order, at the Naval Postgraduate School's MOVES Institute, Fort Ord, and Emeryville.

AEC: The Army Experience Center, a combination of five army recruiting centers with a video game arcade and activity center, was located in the Franklin Mills Mall in Philadelphia, Pennsylvania.

crunch time: An unspecified period of time in game development work that most typically leads up to a release or update of software. Work hours are usually drastically increased to the point that many are forced to neglect social and family obligations to stay at work late or even overnight.

DCS: Digital Consulting Services was the employer of most of the game developers working on *America's Army* in California.

FPS: First-person shooter refers to a genre of video games in which the gamer primarily or exclusively plays from a first-person perspective within a 3D environment. The most visible representation of the gamer is typically a gun, and the most common means of play is shooting at targets—human, alien, and so on—in armed combat. A subset of the FPS genre is the military-themed FPS game. It is becoming more common for FPS games to offer a single-player narrative game, in which combat takes place against a computer opponent, alongside an online multiplayer option, which enables gamers to play against human opponents in arena matches. *America's Army* is an anomaly in this trend, offering no single-player narrative outside of basic training, and the majority of gameplay happens in online or locally networked multiplayer combat.

"honor": A unit of measurement and prestige that was given to player-characters within the online game of *America's Army*, typically ranging from 0 to 99. "Honor" is an aggregate of many numbers and is a generic indicator that measures the skill of players, the length of time a player has played as a specific character, and the ability or willingness of a player to conform to the rules of engagement (ROE) in the game. Players who commit more ROE violations on a regular basis generally have less "honor," as do newer and less skilled players.

Ignited: The Los Angeles–based marketing agency for the *America's Army* franchise, which was responsible for the promotional advertisement for the online game, as well as the design, implementation, and production of both the Virtual Army Experience and the Army Experience Center.

MOS: Military Occupational Specialty.

MOVES Institute: The Modeling, Virtual Environments, and Simulation Institute at the Naval Postgraduate School in Monterey, California, was started by Mike Zyda and was the first development studio of *America's Army*.

NPS: Naval Postgraduate School, in Monterey, California.

OEMA: The Office of Economic and Manpower Analysis, located in the U.S. Military Academy (West Point) Department of Social Sciences; the direct military supervising office for all projects related to *America's Army*, including those located at the SED.

ROE: rules of engagement.

SAIC: Science Applications International Corporation, a large military contractor that was the "prime" contractor for *America's Army*. In 2013 SAIC split into two companies, Leidos and a new company that retains the name SAIC.

SED: Software Engineering Directorate, a U.S. government entity located at Redstone Arsenal, Alabama, which oversaw the project management of the Army Game Project, including projects such as government trainers, the Virtual Army Experience, and the *America's Army* video game.

SME: subject matter expert, typically a soldier (noncommissioned officer or one of higher rank) who advises civilians about specific aspects of the military. In the case of the VAE, SMEs are essentially tour guides and hired employees of Ignited who have been enlisted in the army. In the case of *America's Army* and other Army Game Project training tools, senior enlisted SMEs advised game developers regarding the content and presentation of the game.

VAE: The Virtual Army Experience, a mobile mission simulator that travels throughout the United States.

Virtual Heroes: Located in Raleigh, North Carolina, and now owned by Applied Research Associates, Virtual Heroes was previously an independent company and the development studio for the *America's Army* Government Applications contract. Virtual Heroes contributed to the development of *Moonbase Alpha*, a NASA-funded free-to-play public simulation. The company, which has emerged as a leading serious games developer, works on additional projects for U.S. government organizations, such as the FBI, by using the Unreal game engine (the same engine used by *America's Army*) to develop government training simulations.

Zombie Studios: Zombie Studios, now closed, was a Seattle-based studio that regularly worked as a subcontracted developer on Army Game Project material (the VAE and *America's Army 3*) and other Department of Defense projects (e.g., *Future Force Company Commander*), in addition to developing independent commercial games.

References

Achter, Paul. 2010. "Unruly Bodies: The Rhetorical Domestication of Twenty-First-Century Veterans of War." *Quarterly Journal of Speech* 96 (1): 46–68.

Agamben, Giorgio. 2005. *State of Exception*. Translated by Kevin Attell. Chicago: University of Chicago Press.

Allen, Robertson. 2009. "The Army Rolls through Indianapolis: Fieldwork at the Virtual Army Experience." *Transformative Works and Cultures* 1 (2). http://journal.transformativeworks.org/index.php/twc/article/view /80/97, accessed August 15, 2014.

———. 2011. "The Unreal Enemy of America's Army." *Games and Culture* 6 (1): 38–60.

———. 2012. "Games without Tears, Wars without Frontiers." In *War, Technology, Anthropology*, edited by Koen Stroken, 83–93. New York: Berghahn Books.

———. 2013. "Virtual Soldiers, Cognitive Laborers." In *Virtual War and Magical Death: Technologies and Imaginaries for Terror and Killing*, edited by Sverker Finnström and Neil Whitehead, 152–70. Durham: Duke University Press.

———. 2014. "*America's Army* and the Military Recruitment and Management of 'Talent': An Interview with Colonel Casey Wardynski." *Journal of Gaming and Virtual Worlds* 6 (2): 179–91.

———. 2015. "Software and Soldier Life-Cycles of Recruitment, Training, and Rehabilitation." In *"The War of My Generation": American Youth Culture and the War on Terror*, edited by David Kieran, 144–67. New Brunswick NJ: Rutgers University Press.

American Civil Liberties Union. 2008. *Soldiers of Misfortune: Abusive U.S. Military Recruitment and Failure to Protect Child Soldiers*. http://www .aclu.org/pdfs/humanrights/crc_report_20080513.pdf, accessed August 15, 2014.

Army Game Project. 2005. America's Army *Training Manual*. U.S. Army. http://americasarmy.filefront.com/file/Instruction_Manual_

PDF;8203#Download, accessed July 10, 2014 (no longer available online).

———. 2007. "The Virtual Army Experience Launched!" February 12. http:// www.americasarmy.com/intel/article.php?t=248663, accessed April 13, 2008 (no longer available online).

———. 2008. "America's Army Medic Training Helps Save a Life." January 8. http://www.americasarmy.com/intel/article.php?t=271086, accessed April 2, 2008 (no longer available online).

Arquilla, John, and David Ronfeldt, eds. 2001. *Networks and Netwars: The Future of Terror, Crime, and Militancy*. Santa Monica: RAND.

Baudrillard, Jean. 1994. *Simulacra and Simulation*. Translated by Sheila Faria Glaser. Ann Arbor: University of Michigan Press.

———. 1995. *The Gulf War Did Not Take Place*. Sydney: Power Publications.

BBC News. 2009. "What is anti-X Factor song Killing in the Name all about?" BBC. December 18. http://news.bbc.co.uk.nyud.net/2/hi/uk_news /magazine/8419446.stm, accessed July 4, 2014.

———. 2010. "Call of Duty: Modern Warfare 2 takes $1bn in sales." BBC. January 13. http://news.bbc.co.uk/2/hi/technology/8457335.stm, accessed June 26, 2014.

Berardi, Franco "Bifo." 2009a. *Precarious Rhapsody: Semiocapitalism and the Pathologies of the Post-Alpha Generation*. Edited by Erik Empson and Stevphen Shukaitis. Translated by Ariana Bove, Erik Empson, Michael Goddard, Giuseppina Mecchia, and Antonella Schintu. London: Minor Compositions.

———. 2009b. *The Soul at Work: From Alienation to Autonomy*. Translated by Francesca Cadel and Giuseppina Mecchia. Los Angeles: Semiotext(e).

Bickford, Andrew. 2009. "Anthropology and HUMINT." In *The Counter-Counterinsurgency Manual: Or, Notes on Demilitarizing American Society*, 135–51. Chicago: Prickly Paradigm.

Bingham, Amy. 2011. "Pentagon's NASCAR Sponsorship Gets a Green Light: Congress Rejects Measure to Cut Funding for Ads on Race Cars." ABC News. February 18. http://abcnews.go.com/blogs/politics/2011/0 2/pentagons-nascar-sponsorship-gets-a-green-light-congress-rejects -measure-to-cut-funding-for-ads-on-r/, accessed June 26, 2014.

Borges, Jorge Luis. 1998. *Collected Fictions*. New York: Penguin.

Burgess, Lisa. 2008. "Army Reviews Incentive Program to Improve Retention or [*sic*] Captains." *Stars and Stripes*. April 18. http://www.stripes.com /news/army-renews-incentive-program-to-improve-retention-or-cap-tains-1.77789, accessed June 26, 2014.

Card, Orson Scott. 1991. *Ender's Game*. New York: Tor.

Carroll, Jason. 2009. "U.S. Army Video Game Recruiting." CNN. January 14. Online video report. http://www.cnn.com/video/#/video/tech/2009 /01/14/carroll.mall.recruiting.cnn, accessed July 24, 2014.

Chaplin, Heather, and Aaron Ruby. 2005. *Smartbomb: The Quest for Art, Entertainment, and Big Bucks in the Videogame Revolution.* Chapel Hill: Algonquin Books.

Chapman, Adam. 2004. "Bang the Machine: Computer Gaming Art and Artifacts @ Yerba Buena Center for the Arts." *Intelligent Agent* 4 (2) (Spring). http://www.intelligentagent.com/archive/IA4_2reviewbang themachinechapman.pdf, accessed July 10, 2014.

Cork, Jeff. 2009. "Modern Warfare Sells Close to 5 Million in First Day." *Gameinformer*. November 12. http://www.gameinformer.com/b/news /archive/2009/11/12/modern-warfare-2-sells-close-to-5-million-in-first -day.aspx, accessed June 26, 2014.

Crogan, Patrick. 2011. *Gameplay Mode: War, Simulation, and Technoculture.* Minneapolis: University of Minnesota Press.

Davis, Margaret, and Phillip Bossant, eds. 2004. *America's Army PC Game Vision and Realization: A Look at the Artistry, Technique, and Impact of the U.S. Army's Groundbreaking Tool for Strategic Communication.* Monterey CA: U.S. Army and MOVES Institute.

Davis, Mike. 1990. *City of Quartz: Excavating the Future in Los Angeles.* London: Verso.

Deleuze, Gilles. 1992. "Postscript on the Societies of Control." *October* 59 (Winter): 3–7.

Denvir, Daniel. 2008. "Philly's Military Amusement Park." *Free Speech Radio News.* November 13. http://archive.fsrn.org/audio/newscast-thursday -november-13-2008/5309, accessed July 24, 2014; see also http://www .phillyimc.org/en/phillys-military-amusement-park, accessed July 24, 2014.

Department of Defense, Office of Inspector General. 2005. "Development and Management of the Army Game Project." Report No. D-2005-103. http:// www.dodig.mil/Audit/reports/FY05/05-103.pdf, accessed August 15, 2014.

Der Derian, James. 2001. *Virtuous War: Mapping the Military-Industrial-Media-Entertainment Network.* Boulder: Westview Press.

———. 2003. "War as a Game." *The Brown Journal of World Affairs* 10 (1): 37–48.

Dunnigan, James. 1992. *The Complete Wargames Handbook: How to Play, Design, and Find Them.* Revised edition. New York: Quill.

Dyer-Witheford, Nick, and Grieg De Peuter. 2005. "A Playful Multitude?

Mobilising and Counter-Mobilising Immaterial Game Labour." *Fibrecul-
ture* 5. http://www.journal.fibreculture.org/issue5/depeuter_dyerwith
eford.html, accessed August 15, 2014.

———. 2009. *Games of Empire: Global Capitalism and Video Games*. Minneapolis: University of Minnesota Press.

Eco, Umberto. 1986. "Travels in Hyperreality." In *Faith in Fakes*, translated by
William Weaver. London: Secker and Warburg.

Edery, David, and Ethan Mollick. 2009. *Changing the Game: How Video Games
Are Transforming the Future of Business*. Upper Saddle River NJ: Pearson
Education.

Eisenhower, Dwight D. 1961. "Text of the Address by President Eisenhower."
White House press release. January 17. Published online by the Dwight D.
Eisenhower Presidential Library. http://www.eisenhower.archives.gov
/research/online_documents/farewell_address/1961_01_17_Press
_Release.pdf, accessed May 13, 2014.

Enloe, Cynthia. 2000. *Maneuvers: The International Politics of Militarizing
Women's Lives*. Berkeley: University of California Press.

Entertainment Software Association (ESA). 2008. *Essential Facts about the
Computer and Video Game Industry: 2008 Sales, Demographic, and Usage
Data*. http://www.theesa.com/facts/pdfs/esa_ef_2008.pdf, accessed
May 1, 2014.

———. 2014. *Essential Facts about the Computer and Video Game Industry:
2014 Sales, Demographic, and Usage Data*. http://www.theesa.com/wp
-content/uploads/2014/10/ESA_EF_2014.pdf, accessed October 9, 2015.

———. 2015. *Essential Facts about the Computer and Video Game Industry:
2015 Sales, Demographic, and Usage Data*. http://www.theesa.com/wp
-content/uploads/2015/04/esa-Essential-Facts-2015.pdf, accessed
October 9, 2015.

Faylor, Chris. 2009. "America's Army Devs Laid Off Following Launch
(Updated)." *Shacknews*. June 18. http://www.shacknews.com/article
/59202/americas-army-devs-laid-off, accessed August 15, 2014.

Federal Bureau of Investigation. 2015. "2014 Crime in the United States."
https://www.fbi.gov/about-us/cjis/ucr/crime-in-the-u.s/2014/crime-in
-the-u.s.-2014/tables/table-1, accessed January 31, 2016.

Feldman, Allen. 2004. "Deterritorialized Wars of Public Safety." In *State,
Sovereignty, War: Civil Violence in Emerging Global Realities*, edited by
Bruce Kapferer, 16–28. New York: Berghahn Books.

Fish Software. 2007. "Case Study: Fish Supports the U.S. Army Virtual Army
Experience." http://www.fishsoftware.com/clients/vae.htm, accessed
August 13, 2008 (no longer available online).

Fogg, B. J. 2003. *Persuasive Technology: Using Computers to Change What We Think and Do*. San Francisco: Morgan Kaufmann.

Foucault, Michel. 1992. *The History of Sexuality: An Introduction*. Vol. 1. Translated by Robert Hurley. New York: Vintage Books.

Freedman, Paul. 2013. *Halfway Home*. Documentary film. Los Angeles: GoDigital.

Fricker, Ronald, and Christine Fair. 2003. *Going to Malls to Look for Diamonds: Experimenting with Military Recruiting Stations in Malls*. Santa Monica: RAND.

Gilmore, Ruth Wilson. 2007. *Golden Gulag: Prisons, Surplus, Crisis, and Opposition in Globalizing California*. Berkeley: University of California Press.

Goldberger, Paul. 2013. "Exclusive Preview: Google's New Built-From-Scratch Googleplex." *Vanity Fair*. February 22. http://www.vanityfair.com/online /daily/2013/02/exclusive-preview-googleplex?mbid=social_twitter, accessed May 8, 2014.

González, Roberto. 2012. "World in a Bottle: Prognosticating Insurgency in Iraq and Afghanistan." In *War, Technology, Anthropology*, edited by Koen Stroken. New York: Berghahn Books.

Graeber, David. 2004. *Fragments of an Anarchist Anthropology*. Chicago: Prickly Paradigm.

Gray, Anne. 2004. *Unsocial Europe: Social Protection or Flexploitation?* London: Pluto.

Gray, Chris Hables. 1997. *Postmodern War*. New York: Guilford.

———. 2003. "Perpetual Revolution in Military Affairs, International Security, and Information." In *Bombs and Bandwidth: The Emerging Relationship Between Information Technology and Security*, edited by Robert Latham, 199–212. New York: New Press.

———. 2005. *Peace, War, and Computers*. New York: Routledge.

Greenwald, Glenn. 2014. "The Militarization of U.S. Police: Finally Dragged into the Light by the Horrors of Ferguson." *The Intercept*. August 14. https://theintercept.com/2014/08/14/militarization-u-s-police-dragged -light-horrors-ferguson/, accessed September 12, 2015.

Greenwald, Will. 2007. "The Virtual Army Experience: The U.S. Army Brings Virtual to Potential Recruits with Its Touring Virtual Army Experience Exhibit." CNET. October 2. http://www.cnet.com/news/the-virtual-army -experience, accessed August 10, 2016.

Gutmann, Matthew, and Catherine Lutz. 2010. *Breaking Ranks: Iraq Veterans Speak Out against the War*. Berkeley: University of California Press.

Halpern, Sue. 2008. "Virtual Iraq: Using Simulation to Treat a New Generation of Traumatized Veterans." *New Yorker*. May 19. http://www.newyork er.com/reporting/2008/05/19/080519fa_fact_halpern, accessed August 13, 2014.

Halter, Ed. 2006. *From Sun Tsu to Xbox: War and Video Games*. New York: Thunder's Mouth Press.

Hamacher, Heather. 2007. "'America's Army' Contractors Take Basic Train- ing." *Army News Service*. November 15. http://www.army.mil/article /6131/americas-army-contractors-take-basic-combat-training, accessed August 15, 2014.

Harari, Oren. 2002. *The Leadership Secrets of Colin Powell*. New York: McGraw Hill.

Hardt, Michael, and Antonio Negri. 2000. *Empire*. Cambridge MA: Harvard University Press.

———. 2004. *Multitude: War and Democracy in the Age of Empire*. New York: Penguin.

Herman, Edward, and Noam Chomsky. 2002 [1988]. *Manufacturing Consent: The Political Economy of the Mass Media*. New York: Random House.

Herz, J. C. 1999. *Joystick Nation: How Videogames Ate Our Quarters, Won Our Hearts, and Rewired Our Minds*. Boston: Little, Brown.

Herz, J. C., and Michael R. Macedonia. 2002. "Computer Games and the Military: Two Views." *Defense Horizons* 11 (April): 1–8.

Hodes, J., and E. Ruby-Sachs. 2002. "*America's Army* Targets Youth." *The Nation*. September 2. http://www.thenation.com/article/americas-army -targets-youth, accessed August 15, 2014.

Hoffman, Danny. 2011. *The War Machines: Young Men and Violence in Sierra Leone and Liberia*. Durham: Duke University Press.

Huizinga, Johan. 1950. *Homo Ludens: A Study of the Play Element in Culture*. Boston: Beacon Press.

Jarecki, Eugene. 2005. *Why We Fight*. Documentary film. Los Angeles: Sony Pictures Classics.

Jauregui, Beatrice. 2015. "World Fitness: U.S. Army Family Humanism and the Positive Science of Persistent War." *Public Culture* 27 (3): 449–85.

Jenkins, Henry. 2003. "War Games." *Technology Review*. November 7. http:// www.technologyreview.com/printer_friendly_article.aspx?id=13383, accessed May 6, 2014.

———. 2004. "The War Between Effects and Meaning: Rethinking Video Game Violence." *Independent Schools*. Spring.

———. 2005. "Games, the New Lively Art." In *Handbook for Video Game Studies*, edited by Jeffrey Goldstein, 175–89. Cambridge MA: MIT Press.

Klein, Naomi. 2008. *The Shock Doctrine: The Rise of Disaster Capitalism*. New York: Picador.

Kline, Stephen, Nick Dyer-Witherford, and Greig De Peuter. 2003. *Digital Play: The Interaction of Technology, Culture, and Marketing*. Montreal: McGill–Queen's University Press.

Kowert, Rachel, and Thorsten Quandt. 2016. *The Video Game Debate: Unravelling the Physical, Social, and Psychological Effects of Digital Games*. New York: Routledge.

Kucinich, Dennis. 2009. "Eliminate Deceptive Army Recruitment." Press release from the office of U.S. congressman Dennis Kucinich. March 12. http://www.commondreams.org/newswire/2009/03/12-6, accessed July 4, 2014.

Larkin, Erik. 2005. "U.S. Army Invades E3." *PC World*. May 23. http://www.pcworld.com/article/120929/article.html, accessed July 10, 2014.

Lawson, Sean, Hector Postigo, and Marouf Hasian. 2007. "A Hopeful Mirror: Military Games as Visions of the Future Army." Presented at the Society for Social Studies of Science annual conference, Montreal, October 11–13.

Lazzarato, Maurizio. 1996. "Immaterial Labour." Translated by Paul Coilli and Ed Emory. In *Radical Thought in Italy Today*, edited by Michael Hardt and Paolo Virno, 133–47. Minneapolis: University of Minnesota Press.

Leland, John. 2009. "Urban Tool in Recruiting by the Army: An Arcade." *New York Times*. January 4. http://www.nytimes.com/2009/01/05/us/05army.html, accessed July 24, 2014.

Lenoir, Timothy. 2000. "All but War Is Simulation: The Military-Entertainment Complex." *Configurations* 8 (3): 289–335.

———. 2003. "Programming Theaters of War: Gamemakers as Soldiers." In *Bombs and Bandwidth: The Emerging Relationship Between Information Technology and Security*, edited by Robert Latham, 175–98. New York: New Press.

———. 2008. "Recycling the Military-Entertainment Complex." Unpublished whitepaper. http://virtualpeace.org/whitepaper.php, accessed May 22, 2014.

Lenoir, Timothy, and Henry Lowood. 2005. "Theaters of War: The Military–Entertainment Complex." In *Collection-Laboratory-Theater: Scenes of Knowledge in the 17th Century*, edited by Jan Lazardzig, Helmar Schramm, and Ludger Schwarte, 427–56. Berlin: Walter de Gruyter.

Levitt, Steven, and Stephen Dubner. 2005. *Freakanomics: A Rogue Economist Explores the Hidden Side of Everything*. New York: HarperCollins.

Li, Zhan. 2003. "The Potential of America's Army the Video Game as Civilian-Military Public Sphere." MA thesis, Department of Comparative Media Studies, MIT. http://www.gamecareerguide.com/features/230/masters_thesis_the_potential_of_.php, accessed August 15, 2014; http://dspace

.mit.edu/bitstream/handle/1721.1/39162/55872555.pdf, accessed
August 15, 2014.

Loewen, James. 2007. *Lies My Teacher Told Me: Everything Your American History Textbook Got Wrong*. 2nd ed. New York: Touchstone.

Long, Dustin. 2012. "U.S. Army to Discontinue NASCAR Sponsorship in 2013." *USA Today*. November 7. http://usatoday30.usatoday.com/sports/motor /nascar/story/2012-07-10/Army-wont-return-to-NA-SCAR-in-2013/56126666/1, accessed July 2, 2014.

Los Angeles Times Editorial Board. 2013. "California's Prison Mess." *Los Angeles Times*. August 9. http://www.latimes.com/opinion/editorials/la-ed -prison-release-california-jerry-brown-20130809-story.html, accessed May 12, 2014.

Lutz, Catherine. 2001. *Homefront: A Military City and the American 20th Century*. Boston: Beacon Press.

———. 2006. "Empire Is in the Details." *American Ethnologist* 33 (4): 593–611.

———. 2009. "The Military Normal: Feeling at Home with Counterinsurgency in the United States." In *The Counter-Counterinsurgency Manual: Or, Notes on Demilitarizing American Society*, 23–37. Chicago: Prickly Paradigm.

McCarthy, Cormac. 2010 [1985]. *Blood Meridian, or The Evening Redness in the West*. 25th anniversary edition. New York: Vintage Books.

McLay, Robert. 2012. *At War with PTSD: Battling Post-Traumatic Stress Disorder with Virtual Reality*. Baltimore: Johns Hopkins University Press.

McWhertor, Michael. 2009. "America's Army 3 Devs Let Go Day After Launch." *Kotaku*. June 18. http://kotaku.com/5296131/americas-army-3 -devs-let-go-day-after-launch, accessed August 15, 2014.

Meider, Wolfgang. 1993. "'The Only Good Indian Is a Dead Indian': History and Meaning of a Proverbial Stereotype." *The Journal of American Folklore* 106 (419): 38–60.

Meunier, Nathan. 2008. "Vets Protest America's Army Tournament." *The Escapist*. December 8. http://www.escapistmagazine.com/news/view /87943-Vets-Protest-Americas-Army-tournament, accessed July 3, 2014.

Nader, Laura. 1972. "Up the Anthropologist—Perspectives Gained from Studying Up." In *Reinventing Anthropology*, edited by Dell Hymes, 284–311. New York: Pantheon.

National Commission on Terrorist Attacks. 2004. *The 9/11 Commission Report*. New York: W. W. Norton.

National Research Council. 1997. *Modeling and Simulation: Linking Entertainment and Defense*. Washington DC: National Academy Press.

Nieborg, David. 2005. *Changing the Rules of Engagement: Tapping into the*

Popular Culture of America's Army, *The Official U.S. Army Computer Game.*
MA thesis, Faculty of Arts, Utrecht University. http://www.scribd.com
/doc/50778558/63/Tapping-into-the-Popular-Culture-of-Ameri-
ca%E2%80%99s-Army, accessed August 15, 2014.

————. 2009. "Empower Yourself, Defend Freedom!—Playing Games During
Times of War." In *Digital Material: Anchoring New Media in Daily Life and
Technology*, edited by Van den Boomen et al., 35–48. Amsterdam: Amster-
dam University Press.

Nordstrom, Carolyn. 1998. "Deadly Myths of Aggression." *Aggressive Behavior*
24: 147–59.

————. 2004. *Shadows of War: Violence, Power, and International Profiteering
in the Twenty-First Century*. Berkeley: University of California Press.

————. 2007. *Global Outlaws: Crime, Money, and Power in the Contemporary
World*. Berkeley: University of California Press.

Pappalardo, Joe. 2010. "The Rise of the Joystick Army." *Popular Mechanics*.
May 20. http://www.popularmechanics.com/technology/military
/weapons/crows-and-the-joystick-army, accessed July 21, 2014.

Parikka, Jussi. 2014. "Cultural Techniques of Cognitive Capitalism: Metapro-
gramming and the Labour of Code." *Cultural Studies Review* 20 (1): 30–52.

Pasanen, Tero. 2009. "The Army Game Project—Creating an Artefact for
War." MA thesis, Department of Art and Culture Studies, University of
Jyväskylä. https://jyx.jyu.fi/dspace/bitstream/handle/123456789/20128
/URN_NBN_fi_jyu-200905151595.pdf?sequence=1, accessed August 15,
2014.

Pham, Alex. 2002. "Army's New Message to Young Recruits: Uncle 'Sim'
Wants You." *Los Angeles Times*. May 22. PDF image available online at
http://www.movesinstitute.org/~zyda/Press/LATimes22May2002.pdf,
accessed July 10, 2014.

Price, David. 2004. *Threatening Anthropology: McCarthyism and the FBI's
Surveillance of Activist Anthropologists*. Durham: Duke University Press.

————. 2008. *Anthropological Intelligence: The Deployment and Neglect of
American Anthropology in the Second World War*. Durham: Duke University Press.

————. 2011. *Weaponizing Anthropology*. Petrolia CA: Counterpunch.

Rutledge, Raquel. 2008. "Army Shuts Down War Game." *Milwaukee Journal
Sentinel*. July 2. http://www.jsonline.com/news/29400594.html,
accessed July 20, 2014.

Saad, Lydia. 2013. "U.S. Crime Is Up, but Americans Don't Seem to Have
Noticed." Gallup.com. October 31. http://www.gallup.com/poll/165653
/crime-americans-seem-noticed.aspx, accessed May 3, 2014.

Sarkeesian, Anita. 2013. *Damsel in Distress—Tropes vs. Women*. Documentary film. *Feminist Frequency*. http://www.feministfrequency.com/2013/03 /damsel-in-distress-part-1/, accessed May 3, 2014.

Schreier, Jason. 2013. "From Halo to Hot Sauce: What 25 Years of Violent Video Game Research Looks Like." *Kotaku*. January 17. http://kotaku.com /5976733/do-video-games-make-you-violent-an-in-depth-look-at-every thing-we-know-today, accessed December 5, 2015.

———. 2015. "Why Most Video Game 'Aggression' Studies are Nonsense." *Kotaku*. August 14. http://kotaku.com/why-most-video-game-aggression -studies-are-nonsense-1724116744, accessed December 5, 2015.

Sherman, Zachary, Scott Brooks, and J. Brown. 2013. "Proving Grounds." *America's Army Graphic Novel* series. Issue 8. San Diego: Idea and Design Works.

Shilling, Russell, Casey Wardynski, and Mike Zyda. 2002. "Introducing Emotion into Military Simulation and Videogame Design: America's Army: Operations and VIRTE." *Proceedings of the GameOn Conference*. London.

Simons, Anna. 1997. *The Company They Keep: Life Inside the U.S. Army Special Forces*. New York: Avon.

Sinclair, B. 2009. "*America's Army* Bill: $32.8 million: Government Tallies Total Budget for Free-to-Play First-Person Shooter and Military Recruitment Tool's First Decade of Development." *GameSpot*. December 8. http://www.gamespot.com/articles/americas-army-bill-328-million /1100-6242635, accessed June 26, 2014.

Snider, Mike. 2009. "Video Game Sales Hit Record Despite Downturn." *USA Today*. January 18. http://usatoday30.usatoday.com/tech/gaming/2009 -01-15-video-game-sales_N.htm, accessed May 3, 2014.

Stahl, Roger. 2007. *Militainment, Inc.: Militarism and Pop Culture*. Documentary film. Northampton MA: Media Education Foundation.

———. 2010. *Militainment, Inc.: War Media, and Popular Culture*. New York: Routledge.

Steele, Dennis. 2001. *The ARMY Magazine Hooah Guide to Army Counterinsurgency: A 30-Minute Course on the Army's 30-Year Overhaul*. The Association of the U.S. Army. http://www.ausa.org/publications/armymagazine /archive/2007/7/Documents/Steele_COIN_0707.pdf, accessed May 25, 2014.

Terranova, Tiziana. 2000. "Free Labor: Producing Culture for the Digital Economy." *Social Text* 18 (2): 33–58.

Thierer, Adam. 2009. "Video Games and 'Moral Panic.'" *The Technology

Liberation Front. January 23. http://techliberation.com/2009/01/23
/video-games-and-moral-panic/, accessed July 3, 2014.

Turner, Victor. 1967. "Betwixt and Between: The Liminal Period in *Rites de Passage*." In *Forest of Symbols: Aspects of Ndembu Ritual*. Ithaca: Cornell University Press.

Turse, Nick. 2008. *The Complex: How the Military Invades Our Everyday Lives*. New York: Metropolitan Books.

U.S. Army. 2007. *The U.S. Army and Marine Corps Counterinsurgency Field Manual*. Chicago: University of Chicago Press.

U.S. Bureau of Labor Statistics. 2010. "Local Area Unemployment Statistics." http://data.bls.gov/timeseries/LASST060000000000003, accessed August 15, 2014.

U.S. Congress. 2010. *National Defense Authorization Act for Fiscal Year 2010*.

————. 2011. *Armed Forces, U.S. Code 10*. http://www.gpo.gov/fdsys/pkg /CPRT-112HPRT67344/pdf/CPRT-112IIPRT67344.pdf, accessed July 3, 2014.

U.S. General Accounting Office. 2003. "Military Recruiting: DOD Needs to Establish Objectives and Measures to Better Evaluate Advertising's Effectiveness." GAO-03-1005. http://www.gao.gov/new.items/d03100 5.pdf, accessed April 15, 2014.

Virilio, Paul. 1989. *War and Cinema: The Logistics of Perception*. London: Verso.

Virilio, Paul, and Sylvère Lotringer. 1983. *Pure War*. Translated by Mark Polizzotti. New York: Semiotext(e).

Virno, Paolo. 2004. *A Grammar of the Multitude*. Los Angeles: Semiotext(e).

Wardynski, Casey. 1995. "The Labor Economics of Information Warfare." *Military Review*. (May–June): 56–65.

————. 2007. "v3.0 Game Requirements." Unpublished document. Power-Point provided by an *America's Army* producer to Robertson Allen in October 2009.

————. 2009. "Army Game Project Results Overview." Unpublished document. Manuscript provided by Wardynski to Robertson Allen on May 26, 2009.

Wardynski, Casey, David Lyle, and Michael Colarusso. 2009. *Towards a U.S. Army Officer Corps Strategy for Success: A Proposed Human Capital Model Focused upon Talent*. Carlisle PA: Strategic Studies Institute.

Weeks, Kathi. 2011. *The Problem with Work: Feminism, Marxism, Antiwork Politics, and Postwork Imaginaries*. Durham: Duke University Press.

Wells, H. G. 1913. *Little Wars: A Game for Boys from Twelve Years of Age to*

*Hundred and Fifty and for That More Intelligent Sort of Girls Who Like Boys'
Games and Books*. London: Palmer.

Whitehead, Neil, and Sverker Finnström, eds. 2013. *Virtual War and Magical
Death: Technologies and Imaginaries for Terror and Killing*. Durham: Duke
University Press.

Williams, Brian. 2009. "Gamers, the Army Wants YOU." NBC *Nightly News*.
January 7. http://archives.nbclearn.com/portal/site/k-12/flatview?cue
card=39820, accessed July 24, 2014.

Wright, Evan. 2004. *Generation Kill: Devil Dogs, Iceman, Captain America, and
the New Face of American War*. New York: Putnam.

Zyda, Michael. 2002. "Weapons of Mass Distraction: America's Army Recruits
for the Real War." Presentation at the Naval War College Strategic Studies
Group, Newport RI, December 9. http://www.movesinstitute.org/~zyda
/Presentations.html, accessed August 15, 2014.

———. 2004. "Crossing the Chasm Panel." Presented at the Serious Game
Workshop, Game Developers Conference, San Jose, March 23. http://
www.movesinstitute.org/~zyda/Presentations.html, accessed August 15,
2014.

Zyda, Michael, Alex Mayberry, Jesse McCree, and Margaret Davis. 2005.
"From Viz-Sim to VR to Games: How We Built a Hit Game-Based Simula-
tion." In *Organizational Simulation: From Modeling & Simulation to Games
& Entertainment*, edited by W. B. Rouse and K. R. Boff, 553–90. New York:
Wiley.

Index

first-person shooter (FPS), 5–6, 8–10, 13–15, 20, 45, 65–66, 97, 122, 141. *See also* video games
flexploitation. *See* work-play binary
Fogg, B. J., 31, 51, 53
Fordism, 31–32, 41, 42, 80, 114
Foucault, Michel, 28–30
FPS. *See* first-person shooter (FPS)
free labor, 27. *See also* beta testing; immaterial labor
Full Spectrum Warrior, 122, 125. *See also* Institute for Creative Technologies (ICT)

Game Developers Conference, 56, 127, 161
games. *See* interactive media; video games
gamification, 21
Generation Kill, 151, 162
globalization, 25, 29, 33
Graeber, David, 144–45
Grant, John, 97, 112–14
Guinness world records, 7
Gulf War (1991). *See* Persian Gulf War (1991)

Halfway Home, 81, 86
Halter, Ed, 127
Hardt, Michael, 118. *See also* empire
heroification, 87, 97
Herz, J. C., 124
Homefront, 65
Hussein, Saddam, 6, 14

ICT. *See* Institute for Creative Technologies (ICT)
Ignited, 8, 91, 99, 103, 106, 112, 115, 133, 140, 163, 165
immaterial labor, 32, 33, 36, 37, 41–42, 149–50. *See also* affective labor; cognitive labor; post-Fordism
immersion, 5, 8, 11, 45, 50, 94, 123, 161
Institute for Creative Technologies (ICT), 122, 124–25
institutional power, 30, 33, 50, 63, 75, 79, 114, 163. *See also* disciplinary power
institutions, 7, 11, 18–19, 31–32, 35, 41, 47, 49, 51, 62, 79, 88, 100, 117, 119, 122, 155–56; conformity and, 28–29; control and, 73; crisis of, 29–30; labor and, 42, 151, 166; militarization and, 33, 37, 108, 115, 155; normalization of, 61–62; racism and, 30; research within, 11, 16, 163; rivalries within, 39–40, 119, 131–46; total, 31, 80; violence and, 25; war and, 25, 81, 83. *See also* Foucault, Michel; institutional power
interactive media, 6–9, 11, 15, 21, 36–37, 75, 103, 127, 155. *See also* media; video games
interpellation, 26, 50
Iraq War (2003–11), 6, 13–14, 69–71, 73, 78–79, 80, 82–84, 86, 95, 99, 113–14, 128, 148, 151
Iveans, Erich, 115, 138, 141

Jauregui, Beatrice, 106
Jenkins, Henry, 23, 73

Klein, Naomi, 30
knowledge economy, 7, 27, 42. *See also* cognitive labor; immaterial labor; post-Fordism
Kohl, Herb, 122
Kriegsspiel, 119–20
Kucinich, Dennis, 59–60

labor. *See* affective labor; Fordism; immaterial labor; post-Fordism

The Last Starfighter, 125

Leidos. *See* Science Applications International Corporation (SAIC)

Lenoir, Timothy, 116

Li, Zhan, 116

Lieberman, Joseph, 122

liminality, 23, 66, 77, 149, 155

Lockheed Martin, 137

Loewen, James, 87

Long, Mark, 93, 116, 121–22

Lutz, Catherine, 35, 74–75, 145

Macedonia, Michael, 124

Marine Doom, 122

Marxism, 33

masculinity, 20, 31, 36, 64, 87, 102, 120

massively multiplayer online game (MMOG), 22, 26

Mayberry, Alex, 126, 128–31, 134

McCree, Jessee, 126, 129–31, 134

McLaurin, John, 130

meatspace, 22

Medal of Honor (franchise), 65, 141

media: activism, 91–92; convergence of, 21; effects, 14, 36, 56–57; mass, 31, 50, 75; as scapegoat, 14, 61. *See also* interactive media; video games

mediation, 22, 24, 72, 110, 155, 164

Microsoft Flight Simulator, 46

militainment, 24. *See also* military entertainment complex

militarization, 10–12, 24, 28, 31, 33–37, 42, 88, 91, 108–13, 128, 149–51, 155, 157, 161, 164, 166; community and, 109; definition of, 33, 35–36; and demilitarization, 36; of police, 30; of public space, 30. *See also* Enloe, Cynthia

military entertainment complex, 34–36, 61, 99–100, 115–24, 144, 145, 153

military industrial complex, 34, 120, 145

military normal, 35, 61, 155. *See also* Lutz, Catherine

Military Occupational Specialty (MOS), 40, 58, 77, 94, 103, 143

military recruitment: attrition of, 9; costs of, 9, 133; "hard sell" of, 91, 104, 106; inequality and, 108; institutionalization of, 48–49; legacy model of, 11, 51–52; schools and, 43–44, 106–9; "soft sell" of, 33, 76, 88, 91, 102, 104–5, 112, 114, 155; "talent" and, 40–43, 45, 62, 80, 146; virtual, 76–77, 100

MIME-NET, 34. *See also* military entertainment complex

MMOG. *See* massively multiplayer online game (MMOG)

Moonbase Alpha, 141

MOS. *See* Military Occupational Specialty (MOS)

MOVES Institute, 125–26, 128–32, 136

NASCAR, 8, 51, 77, 90, 93

NATO (North Atlantic Treaty Organization), 73, 165

Naval Postgraduate School (NPS), 125, 129, 131–32

Negri, Antonio, 118. *See also* empire

netwar, 118, 145. *See also* Arquilla, John; Ronfeldt, David

the network, 7–9, 18, 20–21, 25, 27, 31–32, 34, 117–19, 145, 155, 164. *See also* Hardt, Michael; Negri, Antonio; netwar

new media. *See* interactive media; media; video games

To order or obtain more information on these or other University of Nebraska Press titles, visit nebraskapress.unl.edu.

CPSIA information can be obtained
at www.ICGtesting.com
Printed in the USA
LVHW032153260622
722159LV00004B/286

9 781496 201911